A History of the Early Church

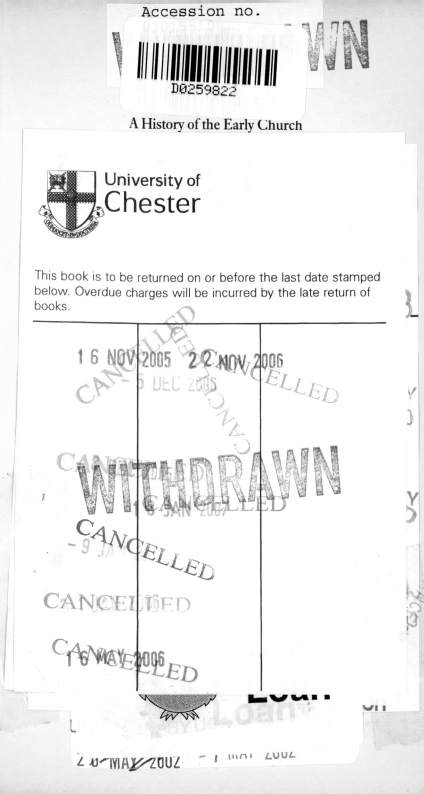

University of Chester

This book is to be returned on or before the last date stamped below. Overdue charges will be incurred by the late return of books.

A HISTORY OF THE EARLY CHURCH

Norbert Brox

SCM PRESS LTD

Translated by John Bowden from the fourth edition
of the German *Kirchengeschichte des Altertums*,
published 1992 by Patmos Verlag, Düsseldorf.

0 334 02576 1

First British edition published 1994
by SCM Press Ltd,
26–30 Tottenham Road, London N1 4BZ

Typeset at The Spartan Press Ltd, Lymington, Hants
and printed in Great Britain by
Biddles Ltd, Guildford and King's Lynn

Contents

Preface

Church history is part of theology. That has not always been taken for granted, as it is today. Certainly it is arguable whether and in what sense a concern with church history can itself be called theology. But in the last two centuries of the history of theology it has become clear that it is impossible to know theology without church history. In other words, it must be recognized that Christianity and the church have in many ways come down to us through history. This insight has changed theology.

In form and 'essence', Christianity cannot be either described or understood without a knowledge of the history through which it became what it is. Anyone concerned with theology has to have a thorough knowledge of the Bible, dogma, the creeds and the institutional form of the church, on the basis of church history. Without such knowledge, decisive features of Christianity will not be recognized and theological insight will be impaired. A knowledge of church history can correct idealistic and ideological abstractions in theology; above all, it can help us to follow and interpret the biblical and dogmatic statements about the special normative character of the relationship between faith and history, revelation and historical research in Christianity, as statements about the actual history of humankind.

A basic account of church history must observe certain conventions. In research and teaching, not to mention examinations, certain approaches and criteria for choosing and presenting topics in church history have become established. The present study follows these criteria in its choice and presentation. Such an account can, of course, always be criticized for omitting or failing to do justice to certain topics. But a compromise has to be made between the mass of material and the number of pages available. I hope that I have found a right balance between a survey which is easy to follow and one which is sufficiently detailed, between readability and a compressed account. This volume is meant for study in the strict sense; it also aims to provide basic information on the history of the early church.

Relevant literature is cited at the end of each chapter (or section) so that the reader can discover more about particular topics. General histories of the early church and other reference books are listed at the end. However, on some topics there is not really much of a choice.

I

The Beginnings of the Church

1. The initial situation

The church began in the small groups of friends, relatives and followers of Jesus of Nazareth which continued or re-formed in Galilee and Jerusalem after his death. Where these groups ('communities') already existed before the death of Jesus, they did not dissolve after the depressing experience of his execution; on the contrary, they developed an intensive community life and engaged in striking propaganda activity. There is an unusual reason for this, about which the communities themselves left detailed evidence. The understandable paralysis, anxiety and resignation which had first spread after Jesus' manifest failure and the loss of their rabbi (cf. e.g. Mark 14.27, 50; Luke 24.20f.) unexpectedly turned into a new initial enthusiasm. This was because of a quite unhoped-for experience which they had and to which they bore witness in stories of completely novel encounters which Jesus had with them ('appearances'), and in statements that he had risen from the dead (I Cor.15.3–8; Mark 16.1–8; Matt.28.1–20; Luke 24.1–53, etc.). We can reconstruct the details of what happened and the course of the earliest history of these groups only to a very limited degree because of the distinctiveness, sparseness and fortuitous nature of the sources.

The sources for our knowledge of the earliest Christian period are the New Testament writings, i.e. a series of testimonies from these Christian communities. For the later decades around the end of the first century and beginning of the second we have a few other works, also Christian, which were not included in the biblical canon; they too contain valuable information (the so-called 'Apostolic Fathers', see Chapter VII below). There is no non-Christian or even archaeological evidence which provides direct information about the earliest period. The content of the historical information given in the earliest Christian writings must always be tested by appropriate methods, as their primary tendency lies on the level of confession and propaganda, not exact historiography.

As a result we know relatively much about the content of the faith and the theologies which were developed in the earliest communities from the recollection of the life and preaching of Jesus and under the impact of his death and the Easter experience. But important historical developments or facts can also be recognized in them or reconstructed from them. Thus geographical information in the New Testament indicates that we must not imagine earliest Christianity from the beginning as an original community only in the city of Jerusalem, but must think of a number of communities which were geographically dispersed, with their local recollections and stories of Jesus, some of which have found their way into our four Gospels. One clear example is the early Easter tradition of appearances of the Risen Jesus in Galilee (as well as Jerusalem, Mark 14.28; 16.7). Such information about locations in early biblical narratives is sometimes a sign that there was a community in the place concerned at a very early stage, which preserved the memory of Jesus contained in the text.

The basic mood of earliest Christianity was an enthusiastic experience of newness, of now experiencing the dawn of the world's salvation. People felt that the 'last days' had dawned, because the Jewish view was that the intervention of God and the creation of the 'new earth' meant the end of the world. So Christians (like some contemporary Jews) lived in an apocalyptic expectation of the end of the world. This was expected very soon, along with dramatic human and cosmic catastrophes (Mark 13). The kingdom of God urgently proclaimed by Jesus (Mark 1.15) could not be long in coming. Jesus himself had announced it for the immediate future (Mark 9.1). Furthermore, now the crucified Jesus had already returned to the world of the living as the firstfruit of the dead; for the Jewish thought of the time, that could only mean the beginning of the end.

This imminent expectation which realistically reckoned with a speedy end to the world may have disappeared during the course of the first century, but as long as it was alive, and even afterwards, it determined all perspectives and interests, and even the intensity of belief and action. So from the second century on, the earliest Christian communities still looked very different from the later church. There were small groups which still had no institutional rules; in other words, their prime concern was not with structures of order and ministries with particular competences. They did not establish their own organized religious association because they did not think long-term institutions necessary. What they thought necessary was a real conversion from life as previously lived, a farewell to demons (gods), baptism as liberation from death-dealing sin, and along with this membership of a community in which the commemorative meal of the end time was celebrated. This brought fellowship with the Risen Jesus and thus with the only true and saving God, so that the second coming (*parousia*) of the Redeemer and judgment could confidently be expected as salvation (cf. I Thess.1.9f.). As the communities thus judged that the world and history had already run their course, and at the same time were convinced that in the gospel they had the only knowledge which was crucial for all humankind, for the space of time that was left they concentrated on the one hand on radically adapting their individual and communal life to these new circumstances, and on the other on recruiting and helping to save as many people as possible who were still living in ignorance or error. For them, all reality was divided into old and new. From the old, in other words the present age and world, they expected nothing new. But the old continued to resist God vigorously, would not be converted, and persecuted the 'saints', as the Christians called themselves because of their election. This gave rise to a situation of confrontation and combat which could be described in both mythical (demons, the devil, enemies of God) and moral (blasphemy, sin, unbelief) terms.

These basic trends in the way in which the earliest Christians understood themselves had obvious consequences for the social behaviour of such small groups and led them deliberately and consistently into a (provisional) social isolation (see Chapter III, 1). They represented merely a tiny, insignificant minority in society, with no real prospect of success and recognition, strictly intent on moral and religious separation. Nevertheless these communities were driven on by the firm conviction that the decisive world event was taking place in their midst. The turning point in the history of the world from hopelessness to salvation for all humankind had begun in the community. These small groups understood themselves to be the centre of world history. Their concept of their own significance stood in crude contrast to their social and sociological insignificance. The stronger the pressure and resistance from outside became, the firmer this self-understanding was.

So we can understand why there was no concern here for permanent institutions and stable structures. The need for order, discipline and responsibility certainly also made itself felt in earliest Christianity; however, the pragmatic measures or rules which, for example, Paul aimed at in some of his letters did not yet have the character of legal church order as it later took shape, but were primarily concerned with the development of gifts (charisms) in the community and in maintaining a Christian ethos (I Cor.12.4–30). (For the history of church order see Chapter IV, 2.)

2. Earliest Christianity in Judaism

Thus the first communities were groups that formed within Judaism in Palestine. In any case Judaism already consisted of different religious parties, so that a new trend (within Judaism) was not in itself either a sensation or a scandal. Christians believed as before in the God of Israel: their Bible was the Bible of Jews (but interpreted in a new way). That they attached their messianic faith and their apocalyptic expectation to Jesus of Nazareth did not make them intolerable deviants within Judaism, which – apart from its biblical monotheism and the obligation to observe the Law – was relatively undogmatic. For they continued to observe (as Jesus did) the Jewish practice of temple worship and law (Acts 2.46; 10.14), and gave outsiders the impression of being a Jewish sect (Acts 24.5, 14; 28.22), not a new religion. They themselves probably also simply thought of themselves as Jews.

However, they lived in accordance with the teaching of the Jew Jesus, who was their only teacher. At a very early stage they also already practised baptism as the rite of acceptance into their community. So they were an independent community. They celebrated the eucharistic meal in their homes as a private liturgical celebration in which only members of the community could take part, though alongside this they continued to practise the Jewish cult.

All this is a clear sign of the independence of this group within Judaism; it shows that it led a life of its own. However, this did not amount to a separation from Judaism. The early church understood itself as an event within Israel. In it God's Spirit of the end time which had been announced to Israel by the prophets (Acts 2.1–21) was starting its activity. It was here that the 'end' of the history of Israel was being played out, in so far as this history was now finding its goal and its fulfilment at the end of the ages. Here earliest Christianity understood itself as the 'new' Israel, in the sense that while it had not replaced the 'old' Israel, as a whole Israel would become this new Israel, i.e. would follow Jesus and come to faith in him. The early community (like Jesus, Mark 7.27; Matt.15.24) saw its task *in* Israel, and initially not beyond it (cf. Matt.10.5f.). From the first day on, it had this universal tendency to represent all Israel instead of forming a 'holy remnant'. For the earliest community, Israel's historical rejection of faith in Jesus was therefore a cruel disillusionment and became a theological problem (Rom.9–11). The early success of mission among the Gentiles then made universalism topical again: it was now related beyond all Israel to 'all nations'.

3. Groups and trends in earliest Christianity

(a) 'Hebrews' and 'Hellenists'

Earliest Christianity was not only dispersed geographically; its basic religious position and practice were not uniform either. The most fundamental distinction concerned the relationship of the community to Judaism. Not all Christians had the same Jewish past. In Judaism itself (even in the Jerusalem synagogues) there was a difference between the indigenous Jews who spoke Aramaic and the Greek-speaking (or bilingual) Jews who had lived abroad in Hellenistic cultures in the Jewish diaspora (e.g. in Egypt, Greece, Asia Minor or Rome). Because they spoke a different language they had formed different synagogue communities. We must also suppose that there were differences among them over their religious relationship to the land of Israel, the temple, worship and the law, which for Jews in the Diaspora could not play the same role as they did in the mother country. Members of the earliest community in Jerusalem came from both groups, so that this division was repeated there. In Acts the two groups of Christians are called 'Hebrews' and 'Hellenists' (Acts 6.1). From this Lukan writing we can infer that they probably formed two Christian communities which separated for worship because of the linguistic barriers, but for example joined together in charitable activity. The group of the Seven from Acts 6.5 with exclusively Greek names (Stephen, Philip, Prochorus, Nicanor, Timon, Parmenas and Nicolaus) probably represent the leaders of the 'Hellenists', a counterpart to the college of apostles for the 'Hebrews'. There were occasionally difficulties between the two groups in the earliest Jerusalem community (Acts 6.1). What was more significant for church history, however, was that the Christian 'Hellenists' became involved in a serious conflict with the Greek-speaking synagogues in the city. This is reflected in the story of Stephen in Acts 6.8–7.60, but certainly extended far beyond this one event involving Stephen. Thus the reason for the clash clearly lay in the teaching of the Christian Hellenists in so far as it related to their view of Judaism. We can see from the sources that this group of Jerusalem Christians was firmly committed to the memory of a particular line of Jesus' preaching, namely the criticism of the temple and the law with which he had attacked the established religious practice and the current understanding of the law in his time (but not Jewish existence as such). Thus according to Luke the charge of the witnesses or the authorities against Stephen was one of 'blasphemy' against Moses, God, the temple and the Law; he was even said to want to abolish the temple and the laws of Moses, referring to 'this Jesus' (Acts 6.11–13; 7.48, 53). The way in which the preaching of the 'Hellenists' relativized and criticized the temple went beyond the limits of what synagogue discipline could tolerate – as had already happened in the case of Jesus. The authorities intervened and drove these Christians from the city as Jewish heretics (Acts 8.1). (This was the first persecution of Christians in history, in which Paul was probably also involved, Gal.1.13.)

Now the two groups in the earliest community were separated by events: the 'Hellenists' had to leave Jerusalem; the 'Hebrews' remained there. So we can see how markedly they must have differed from one another: the 'Hebrews' gave the Jewish authorities no occasion for disciplinary measures. The criticism of the Law had not played a comparable role in their Jesus traditions. On the contrary, they remembered and preached Jesus as the one who had inculcated the Law down to the smallest detail (Matt.5.17–19). The 'Hellenists' may well have been predisposed to be receptive to Jesus' criticism of cult and law by their Jewish past in the Diaspora, where in many instances external conditions could lead to a more liberal and basically open attitude of Jewish faith than could be taken for granted in the mother country. At all events, for them, closeness to the preaching and discipleship of Jesus was more important than closeness to the legal practice of Jewish piety. So here a permanent division took place in early Christianity: the 'Hellenists' felt that as a result of Jesus, the cult and the law were no longer binding; for that they were driven out, not to return. The 'Hebrews' combined their belief in Jesus with their Jewish observance, and continued to be tolerated within the sphere of Judaism, where they had a limited future by being relatively cut off from the rest of church history. Thus even in the second and third centuries there were strong Christian groups in the Near East which practised their Christianity in a very Jewish way: they observed the Law (at least in part), revered Moses as a prophet, and hated and repudiated Paul as a 'traitor' who wanted to 'abolish' the Law.

Furthermore, this *de facto* division of earliest Christianity for a time also led to a serious conflict within the church. In their mission outside Palestine, the 'Hellenists' who had been driven out had practised and preached among the Gentiles a Christianity without Judaism, i.e. without the law and circumcision. Some of the Palestinian Christians who had largely remained Jewish vigorously protested against this, and intervened in places because they were convinced that baptism in the name of Jesus presupposed conversion and obedience to the law. After his conversion Paul found himself involved in this conflict and helped to decide it finally in favour of a mission to the Gentiles which did not preach observance of the Law (Gal.2). In these controversies Peter played more the role of mediator, while James the brother of the Lord, who was the key authority in Jerusalem, argued energetically for the practice there.

This is the setting for the so-called 'Apostolic Council' in the year 48 (Gal.2; Acts 15.1–29), a meeting of representatives of the different earliest Christian groups; this reached agreement that Christianity should be propagated among the Gentiles without Jewish additions, but that among Jews it must continue to be combined with Jewish observance of the Law. At that time the earliest church deliberately decided on different ways for the gospel. Hellenistic Christianity had an unprecedented significance for the further history and expansion of Christianity (see above, I, 4). But that also applies to earliest Jewish Christianity in Jerusalem and Palestine, even on Greek soil. Here belief in Jesus was developed against the background of Jewish faith and thought, and expressed wholly in the categories of the Jewish expectation of salvation. The outline of the gospel of God's revelation and salvation in Jesus of Nazareth, the resultant hope for humankind and the pattern of Christian moral behaviour, had and continued to have a marked Jewish colouring, as quite particularly did the basic forms of Christian liturgy (the liturgy of the word with readings, teaching and prayer; the celebration of a meal and baptism). The earliest Jewish-Christian community also bequeathed these and other essential elements (its understanding of history, revelation and salvation) to Gentile Christianity. However, the transfer was made by the 'Hellenists', who themselves were Jews in origin.

(b) Other trends

The differentiation of earliest Christianity into various trends was not limited to the question of Judaism in Christianity. Different views, terminologies, focal points, similarly developed in many other themes of the confession. For the first decades the New Testament reflects a great variety. For example, we have the Synoptic, the Pauline, the Johannine traditions, each with its individual christology, eschatology, ecclesiology and soteriology. The intensive community life of the small groups was strikingly productive in reflecting and interpreting the faith, usually in very direct connection with the situation and environment of the individual community. One particularly impressive example of this is the Christian group whose existence must be inferred from the source Q, which

Matthew and Luke use for their Gospels. It gave Jesus the apocalyptic name 'Son of Man' and thus lived with an acute expectation of the end; it selected from the words of Jesus that had been remembered predominantly those sayings which call for generosity, mercy, love of enemy, non-violence and love, and for the gathering of 'sons of peace'. These Christians had occasion to retain a vivid memory of these particular words of Jesus, because in Palestine they came into conflict with Jews who at that time were organizing armed resistance against the Roman occupation, resistance which found expression in the First Jewish War of 66–70 CE. They argued against war and were persecuted as collaborators, at any rate in the Second Jewish War of 132–135 CE. Right at the beginning Christianity was lived out in very different situations. The different forms and terminologies in which it is attested historically can be explained from the particular involvement which sparked them off.

4. The early expansion and its characteristics

Christianity already spread in a quite amazing way in its first decades. Within a short time it was in Palestine, Syria, Asia Minor, Cyprus, Greece, Egypt and Rome, though we do not know precisely who brought it to all these places. Travelling missionaries like Paul and his fellow-workers were primarily responsible for these rapid successes; they would leave the communities which they had founded to look after themselves, in order to form new ones elsewhere. In other words, they attempted to cover relatively large areas with a considerable degree of (apocalyptic) haste and restlessness, aiming at only the cities (and the larger ones at that). Paul wanted to get to Spain (Rom.15.24), having preached 'from Jerusalem to Illyria' (present-day Yugoslavia) (15.19).

But it was the 'Hellenists' driven out of Jerusalem (see Chapter I,3, a) who played the fundamental part in the great initial success. It was through them that the gospel was first preached outside Palestine and to non-Jews (Acts 8.4f.; 11.19f.). And they preached a Christianity which did not require acceptance of the law and circumcision. The non-Jewish Christian community in the great Syrian city of Antioch was of special significance. Here *a priori* the

Jewish law did not apply. Reciprocal relations with the synagogue in the city were therefore excluded, so that according to tradition people first called 'the disciples' 'Christians' here (Acts 11.26). It is significant that this Christianity free of the Law was Greek-speaking, and thus could be understood everywhere, in the cities and in part also in the country. These two characteristics of freedom from the Law and the Greek language represented a universal openness of a kind which had never existed before in Aramaic Jewish Christianity with a Palestinian stamp. The further expansion of Christianity during late antiquity (Chapter II) is also conceivable only on these presuppositions. Christianity increasingly became a separate religion alongside Judaism.

It can be seen from the missionary stage from Jerusalem to Antioch (a distance of less than 300 miles), from Palestine to Syria, that the expansion represented not only a quantitative geographical increase in Christianity but also its translation or transformation into new surroundings and cultural spheres. Not only its relationship to Judaism and the Law but other features too were developed or changed here, for example its image of God, its understanding of baptism and eucharist, its christological statements, its idea of the Spirit. Jewish or biblical categories in Christian theology and preaching were exchanged for patterns of thought and imagery which corresponded to the religious tradition of the Gentiles (Gentile Christians) and were more accessible to them. However, one important characteristic remained the freedom of Christians from the ritual and legal tabu of the (Jewish) Law. Paul got to know Christianity in this version, adopted it and helped to impose it on theology and the church. And this law-free gospel won the day.

Not only the geographical and theological perspectives, but also the sociological perspectives in the expansion of earliest Christianity are interesting. From what strata of the population did these people come? A former theory that the earliest community had a proletarian character has proved false. The earliest witnesses show clearly enough that from the beginning people from higher social strata, with some distinction in society, became Christians. To put it in extreme form, Christianity was never a religion of slaves. It seems that the relations between the upper, middle and lower classes in the early church corresponded roughly to those in the society of its time. It is in keeping with such a statement that an individual community, say, in the setting of the port of Corinth, could prove to be socially one-sided (I Cor.1.26f.), and even here there is evidence of minorities: according to Paul, in the Corinthian community there are 'not many educated people, not many influential people, not many from respectable families' – but there are some. Women of all social classes had a much greater significance for the life and mission of the communities than in later times, as is shown simply by the many times in which they are mentioned by name in the letters of Paul alone (cf. e.g. Rom.16.1–17).

The geographical expansion created certain conditions for success. Certainly in Palestine and Asia Minor the communities were quite thick on the ground; however, to begin with Christianity gained a footing only in the major cities along the trade routes, sometimes with considerable distances between them. So despite their successful expansion the communities lived in great isolation and were 'lost in space', scattered throughout 'the world', and minorities wherever they were. In other words they were geographically and socially isolated. Accordingly, they felt themselves to be in 'a foreign land' and in the 'dispersion' (I Peter 1.1; 2.11). Some basic features of earliest Christian theology go back to this extreme situation of the small groups. In an environment which was uninterested and often aggressive (see Chapter III, 1), their ethics, world-view and expectations for the future took on a special profile, with a main interest in detachment from the 'world' and deliverance from disaster or at the end of history.

5. The influences of its surroundings on early Christianity

We cannot understand early Christianity and its history unless we take into account the historical conditions and the circumstances of the time which came to influence it. Its environment was first and foremost Palestinian Judaism in its contemporary, post-biblical form. There were other phenomena in the environment, and it was not long before Christianity in turn became a part of its era, late antiquity. This integration did not remain superficial as far as its influence on Christianity was concerned. Thus from the start

Christianity was a syncretistic (mixed) religion; in other words, it was shaped by religious and cultural influences which did not derive from Christianity. These influences came principally from two spheres which together made up the immediate environment of early Christianity: Hellenistic Judaism and the pagan Roman-Hellenistic world. These played a major part in shaping Christianity.

The influence from Hellenistic Judaism was great because Christianity not only had its origin in Judaism but kept encountering Judaism all over the Mediterranean countries. As Diaspora Judaism, this had spread 'worldwide', with focal points for example in Alexandria and Rome, and as a whole was numerically stronger than the Judaism of Palestine. In the Diaspora it had been far more intensively stamped by the Hellenistic environment than had the Judaism of the mother country, and differed from this in language and profile. The proximity of the church to the synagogue in almost all the cities of the empire resulted not only in reciprocal influences but also in a limited solidarity between Christians and Jews and, of course, also in reciprocal polemic. The solidarity consisted, for example, in the Christian defence of a common religious heritage against outsiders by standing up for the Old Testament against pagan criticism and thus at the same time taking the pressure off Judaism. But the Christians were at the same time beneficiaries, not least in apologetics; they could resort to Jewish counter-arguments as presented in an extensive Jewish propaganda literature to defend themselves against many pagan attacks. This again meant that there was Jewish influence on Christian thought. What was even more important was that because of the needs of Greek-speaking Diaspora Judaism, Greek translations of the Jewish Bible, the Christian 'Old Testament', had been made in pre-Christian and early Christian times, above all the so-called Septuagint. So the Bible was available in a language which could be generally understood. Christianity needed only to make use of it for its liturgical, catechetical and missionary purposes. Now at many points the Greek translation amounted to a Hellenistic interpretation of the Jewish Bible. By using it, early Christianity was further influenced and strengthened in its understanding of the biblical tradition, which in any case had already been changed by Hellenism. The fact that

Christians also learned methods of interpreting the Bible from Jewish scriptural exegetes was another influence in the same direction. Christians took over from Hellenistic Jews like Philo of Alexandria (early first century CE) the method of allegorization, through which a deeper, 'spiritual', 'authentic' meaning of scripture was discovered behind the letters of the Bible. This influence extends from Paul to modern times. At the time of the early church, allegorical interpretation made possible a mediation between the Bible and the philosophical thought-patterns in which Christian theology was conceived. The Judaism of the Diaspora translated biblical Jewish statements into Greek language and Hellenistic thought, and in this way pioneered ways which were to be exceptionally important for early Christianity. Thematically, too, it set standards which were adopted in Christian missionary preaching: the witness to monotheism, an indication of the true way of piety, and the opening up of hope for all human life are the key values of biblical proclamation, to which Christians were then to give Christian content. I have already mentioned the influence in the sphere of the liturgy.

The influences from Graeco-Roman antiquity were quite different. Thus it was a decisive factor that Christianity had to establish a foothold in a political order which made certain religious and totalitarian claims. Christianity came into being at a time when, after occupying the eastern Mediterranean by force of arms, Rome was proclaiming itself the universal and final empire, and when as a result of these same events the overall Graeco-Roman culture of Hellenism was taking comprehensive form in religion, philosophy, forms of state and society, law, economics and trade. At that time political events were being interpreted by the Romans in religious terms as a fulfilment of divine providence in which the Roman order was foreseen as a permanent world order. So here Roman imperial power was given a claim to totality and a religious aura (*Roma aeterna; Pax Romana*). Around the beginning of our era this ideology found a new religious form of expression in the institution of the emperor: with the adoption of Hellenistic political ideas, the emperor was exalted to become the representative of the deity: the political authority was divinized. So-called emperor worship developed from this, bringing with it the political and religious requirement of some form of cultic act by the citizens.

In the future, emperor worship belongs with different degrees of emphasis to the official religion of the state, which mainly consisted in the divine cults of ancient religion. Christianity was confronted with a paganism with religious vitality, not with a morbid, played-out religion (although because of enlightened ideas in poetry and philosophy the traditional views were no longer accepted without question). At all events there were living traditions and indeed innovations in the cultic sphere. Religion dominated private and public life. People lived by the rhythm of religious festivals, and in a world full of divine and demonic powers. Here the state carefully looked after its sacral institutions, temples, priests and cults. For as duty towards the gods, on whom the empire was dependent for its prosperity (*salus publica*), religion was primarily a state matter, one which the state could enforce. Thus one of the most significant features of Roman religion at the time of the emperors was that it was a religion of loyalty. State interests and worship could not be separated. The citizen was expected, and on occasions required, to participate in it. But beyond this duty, the religious convictions and notions were citizens were given a considerable degree of tolerance.

This description of the pagan world has already indicated the problems which arose for Christianity and influenced its development (Chapter III, 1). State religion coincided with public interest in religion as the cultic support for politics, but it did not meet the religious needs of the individual in the same way. Individuals had alternatives to the state cult, above all in the so-called mystery religions, i.e. particular cults of Greek origin (e.g. Eleusinian, Orphic and Dionysian mysteries), which met with a great response at the time of earliest Christianity. In certain ceremonies the individual was accepted into a closed circle of privileged initiates who in cultic ecstasy experienced the vision (*epopteia*) of divine things, as a result of which they gained not only an insight but even entry into the divine world beyond, and in sometimes strange rites experienced divinization – in other words, they became certain of their salvation. Only outlines and a few details of this are known, because these cultic communities imposed a strict arcane discipline on their members – in other words they kept the essentials (rites, cultic formulae, sacred objects and writings, cultic knowledge) secret. The alternative this provided to the anonymous state religion is obvious: here in a rite individuals had their religious needs secretly fulfilled in a quite tangible way within the small compass of an esoterically protected group (the community) and came to possess salvation through the performance of the cult and anticipation of it. Whereas official Roman religion, as the classic ancestral tradition, shaped the world-view and culture of the upper classes, in the mysteries we have more of the religious world of lesser people. Because of its greater religious and emotional attractiveness, it seems to have been felt to be a rival to state religion. At all events, there was mistrust on the part of the state: measures were taken against such secret cults, which were outside public control, and there was polemic very similar to that directed against the Christians.

The attitude of Christians to the mysteries was ambivalent. They dissociated themselves from them with sharp criticism, and described them as a realm in which demons were at work, and so on; however, in so doing at the same time they demonstrated deep sympathies. For religious parallels between the mysteries and Christianity cannot be overlooked or disputed. The structure of the community, the promise of salvation to individuals, a hope which applied to them individually, cultic experience and celebration, and other features represented a notable affinity. And Christians also borrowed some elements, particularly of cultic language, like the term 'mystery', for the cultic act and for the revelation of salvation generally; 'initiation', for acceptance into the community; and also elements of a realistic understanding of the cult or the arcane discipline (see Chapter IV, 4). So there was some influence, even if the dependence of Christianity on the mystery religions (like the significance of the latter generally) was limited.

Christianity had contacts with all these forms of alien religion: with the classic religion of antiquity, the cult of emperor and state, the mysteries or oriental religions. This left deep traces of syncretism (= a fusion of different religious phenomena) in the theology, structures and self-understanding of the early church. Judaism and Christianity were the only religions from this period, old or new, to survive late antiquity.

Bibliography

Norbert Brox, 'Forms of Christianity in the Primitive Church', *Concilium* 1971/7, 33–46

James D. G. Dunn, *The Partings of the Ways*, SCM Press and Trinity Press International 1991

Howard Clark Kee, *Christian Origins in Sociological Perspective*, SCM Press 1980

Gerd Lüdemann, *Earliest Christianity according to the Acts of the Apostles*, SCM Press and Fortress Press 1989

Wayne E. Meeks, *The First Urban Christians*, Yale University Press 1983

Gerd Theissen, *The First Followers of Jesus*, SCM Press (US title *The Sociology of Earliest Palestinian Christianity*, Fortress Press) 1978

II

The History of Mission and Conversion

1. *Christianity begins to spread. Why?*

The newly acquired conviction of earliest Christianity that faith in Jesus Christ represents the only chance of salvation for human beings, no matter where and when they may be living, was the foundation of Christian mission and the motive power for it. Here, because of its apocalyptic view of the world (its expectation of the end), the earliest church was pressurized by the thought that the time before the imminent end of the world might be too short (cf. Matt.10.23), or that the world mission had to achieve its goal before the end could come (Matt.24.14). These and similar notions explain the enormous pressure for expansion in the early church and its missionary consciousness, which was to achieve such success. In the course of history the world-wide aim which was already that of earliest Christian expansion (e.g. Rom.10.18; Matt.28.19; Rev.7.9) was realized to a unique degree. The reason for the success was the special character of Christianity as a religion of redemption. The historical beginning of this expansion is to be seen in the growth of the communities within Palestine (here, of course, numbers like those given in Acts 2.41; 4.4 have only symbolic value). But the quite decisive step to 'world mission' was taken by the Jerusalem 'Hellenists' when after being driven out of the city they went beyond Palestine and preached outside its frontiers (Chapter I, 3,4). The stimulus to this was not a church initiative or organization (on the part of the apostles or the like), but the expulsion of part of the earliest community from Jerusalem. In this way, partly of necessity and partly spontaneously, the expansion was originally set in motion. Names of those engaged in mission outside Judaism which have been handed down are those of 'Hellenists' like Philip, Barnabas and Paul; however, the first missionaries, and indeed most of them, are unknown to us.

However, the early church soon created a very different picture of events for itself. Because the biblical texts Matt.28.19; Mark 16.20; Acts 1.8 describe the world mission as a commission given to the twelve apostles, mission was regarded as a task only of the apostles, and not of the later church. Consequently it was thought that the apostles had fulfilled this mission and brought the gospel 'to the ends of the earth'. That was no longer the task of the present church. The world had long since been decisively changed and prepared for its end, because all had heard the gospel. This widespread legendary notion has overpainted and blotted out the memory of most of the historical facts and the names of those who engaged in what was really early mission history.

2. A geographical account of the spread of Christianity

Following on its amazing initial success, Christianity grew steadily, without any great setbacks or standstills, and in some phases could take enormous steps forward. One of the clear periods of success seems to have come about towards the end of the second century (under Emperor Commodus, 180–192), and another quite special one in the second half of the third century, when Christianity achieved such dimensions that it merits being called a mass movement. No contemporary religion had a comparable history of consolidation. The increasing public reactions to the existence of Christianity (Chapter III, 1, 2) are also to be explained in terms of this success. Any geographical survey of the expansion of Christianity must distinguish different chronological phases, noting the progress made in each. In general, much information is uncertain, because at many points the historical sources are full of gaps, unclear and fortuitous.

We can certainly say that at the end of the first century there were Christian communities in Palestine and Syria, on Cyprus, throughout Asia Minor, in Greece and Rome; Christianity at such an early period is more or less uncertain in Alexandria (in Egypt), Illyria and Dalmatia (later to be Yugoslavia), Gaul and Spain. But quite significant churches had grown up there by the end of the second century. In addition to further local churches in the places just mentioned, in the meantime Christianity had been able to establish communities in eastern Syria, Mesopotamia, Egypt, southern Italy, Gaul, Germany, Spain and especially in North Africa (= present-day Tunisia, Algeria, Morocco and Libya); here the expansion westwards quite evidently was not based in Rome but in the East, especially in Asia Minor. There are good reasons for supposing that there were communities in Trier, Mainz and Cologne at the end of the second century. However, in the second century a loss must also be mentioned. The Jewish Christians in Palestine had been driven out in the First Jewish War (66–70) but then had returned to Jerusalem; however, after the Bar Kokhba revolt, the Second Jewish War against the Romans (132–135), they had to leave the land because, as Jews, they had been circumcised, and all Jews were now banned on pain of death. So for the moment that meant the end of this church. In Palestine, too, from now on there was only Gentile Christianity.

Up to the end of the third century Christianity made considerable gains, not only in extent but also within the areas where it already had a footing. The church of Alexandria, with its distinguished bishops and theologians, became very influential in the regions round about (not least in missionary terms), and now there was an indigenous (Coptic) Christianity in the country areas of Egypt. There was also Christianity in northern Arabia (east of the Jordan). In Syria, the church of Antioch became particularly significant as a result of its theology, through synods there and through its missionary initiatives in Armenia, Mesopotamia and Persia. Evidently at the beginning of the fourth century Armenia had a strong Christianity. In Asia Minor mission continued in country areas. Moreover, Christians could now be found exercising many political functions, which suggests that there was a high proportion of them in the overall population of the cities. The development of Christianity was neither as extensive nor as intensive in Greece. In the Balkans and in the Danube provinces, too, mission does not seem to have progressed very fast. By contrast, the community in Rome had to divide itself, becaue it had grown too large: it is calculated that there were tens of thousands of Christians there. There were now also communities in central and southern Italy, though probably only a few of them. There is evidence of Christianity in northern Italy only in the case of a few cities like Ravenna, Aquileia and Milan. The same is true of Sardinia and Sicily. The African church became one of the greatest particular churches with a highly developed self-esteem. Precise information about Spain, Gaul and Germany is difficult to find. And Britain has also to be taken into account.

It is difficult to give absolute numbers of Christians, since we do not even know the total number of the population of the cities. But the number of Christians at this time will hardly have reached more than half the population anywhere.

The church only lost its minority status in the time of Constantine. We can probably speak of a predominantly Christian population of the empire by the middle of the fifth century, alongside which there were pagan and Jewish minorities. From the fourth century onwards, mission was also carried out on a large scale in the interior. However, because of the new conditions (see Chapter III, 2), in this period the success was comparatively slight. Now it was more fashionable than ever to become a Christian. With the greater opportunities for conversion the church now had pastoral problems. One new development was the mission in Ethiopia and among the Nestorian Christians (see Chapter VIII, 6, 7) as far as the Persian Gulf and northern India. In the fourth century there was Christianity on the lower Danube (= Roumania, Bulgaria). The expansion continued in Yugoslavia and also in Greece. Present-day lower Austria and Upper Italy were covered in the period of the imperial church; the Alpine valleys in the fifth century; and southern Germany at the same time. Now Gaul began to take on significance for the church. On the whole, though, mission continued to be laborious and slow, and the baptism of individuals often marked only the beginning of a mission (instead of its success).

3. Sociological data on mission

Of course contemporary sociological factors also played a role in mission. As a rule people in the Hellenistic world were bonded together in a stable, functioning family structure ruled over in patriarchal fashion by the father of the house; the markedly hierarchical ethos predetermined the role of individual members of the family and largely robbed them of the capacity to make decisions (for example of a social or religious nature). In the Diaspora, Jews who from the beginning had a similarly patriarchal orientation lived in family units of the same kind. This social structure had various consequences for the Christian mission. What is reported in the New Testament and repeated later might happen, namely that a man would 'come to believe with his whole house' (Acts 18.8), as he made the decisions for the whole family including slaves. Or it was particularly difficult to extract individuals from their family ties, which were at the same time both religious and social. In the first instance the Christianization of a family would take place at a stroke, within a single generation, something that had been prepared for by the family bond (cf. I Cor.1.16; Acts 11.14; 16.15, 31–33). Alongside the many conversions of individuals this was a regular phenomenon in mission. But it may have been the case more often in Jewish than in pagan households; in pagan households we frequently find the second consequence. First of all only the women could be won over (thus causing crises for marriages), or only the household servants (and not their masters and mistresses) became Christians; or the house could be Christianized only successively and then perhaps not completely. In this case the family bond was a barrier to mission, because it was difficult for the individual to break away from it. But certainly there were conversions of Gentile families.

Christianity achieved a considerable part of its missionary success at the expense of the Jews. The so-called 'godfearers' and proselytes (Gentiles converted to Judaism) would move from the synagogue to Christianity particularly easily and frequently. Socially they belonged to the middle and upper classes, and thus gave a similar stamp to the image of the mission communities.

Christianity also gained adherents from the upper classes of pagan society in the Hellenistic Roman cities. Rich and poor, prominent and ordinary people are attested as Christians in the sources (cf. Chapter I, 4 for earliest Christianity). What was significant for the social perspective and attractiveness of Christianity was that already in the period before Constantine an ever-increasing number of

Christians were active in middle- and high-ranking political and administrative positions. Educated men, philosophers and historians, also soon became Christians. However, for the most part the middle and lower classes of the urban population made up the Christian community – craftsmen, merchants and slaves.

Even more significant than the sociological composition of the early church as such is the fact that within the communities Christianity could integrate the crude social differences which existed in society without any consequent break-up in these communities. However, social problems underlay many conflicts which in the course of time burdened the church in the form of schisms. Moreover the Christian mission also had its economic presuppositions, concomitant circumstances and consequences. Virtually no research has been done here. But the sociological factor that is significant for early Christianity is not a one-sideness in the composition of communities but the abolition of social frontiers by a new set of values (and at the same time also the absence of social criticism or a concern for social reform in the light of existing social conditions). How insignificant social differences were within the church was demonstrated, for example, by the unconventional way in which slaves and women were given equal status; evidently mission was strikingly successful among them.

4. *Conditions, favourable and unfavourable*

There were some circumstances which made the Christian mission easier and accelerated it, and others which made it more difficult and hindered it. The beginnings did not promise success. The new 'superstition' of a numerically small religious movement from the Jewish people on the eastern margin of the empire who had no political or cultural significance whatsoever in no way met the criteria of a serious religion. Nevertheless there was much to favour its expansion.

The markedly favourable conditions include the Pax Romana, i.e. the stable political situation of the world of the time under the authoritarian regime of the Romans and the effective control of that world exercised by their power, which with the state and the army kept the nations peaceful within safe frontiers and united them in a great administrative system. Together with the excellent network of

Roman roads, which made mobility possible over the great distances within the empire in a way unprecedented for the travelling conditions of the time, this had the great advantage of offering many kinds of communication and movement along safe routes without the hindrance of national frontiers. Christianity also profited from this and spread above all along the main routes.

This world which was united by politics and force of arms was also a cultural entity. In religion and thought (philosophy), Hellenistic culture extended beyond national, ethnic and religious differences to make almost all the empire a unity. That meant that the Christian missionary had the same limitations or problems in communicating Christian teaching everywhere, and faced, or was part of, a relatively uniform world. It was enough for Christianity to translate itself into the language and thought-forms of this one culture to be under-standable 'everywhere'. At the time of the rise of Christianity Greek was spoken as the language of commerce almost everywhere from the Near East to the West. Christianity could be preached in a single language from Palestine to Spain. That especially favoured its rapid expansion. However, another effect was that Christianity became and long remained an urban religion, because the 'world language', Greek, was understood in most parts of the empire only in the cities and not in the country. In the country, between the Euphrates and Gaul, Egypt and Britain, countless vernaculars were spoken. In the West in the second to third centuries Greek was then replaced by Latin, in Egypt by Coptic, and so on. Nevertheless, the advantage described above remained. Christianity then continued to articulate itself for the most part in the two cultural languages of Greek and Latin. That meant that it became bound up with culture and education, and avoided being atomized into many languages; letters could be written and information provided easily, but the lack of understanding of these languages in the country was a great barrier for mission.

The stock of ideas within the political, social and cultural unity of the then world had prompted in contemporaries the notion of a unity of the human race: all human beings belonged together in one whole. Christians took up this notion and combined it with the gospel of the comprehensive salvation of all humankind by the one God and the future unity of the nations.

One reason for the success of the early Christian mission also lies in Judaism. Diaspora Judaism itself carried on an intensive and successful mission. The success of this mission meant that this form of Judaism was in a position to present itself as a universal (and no longer as a narrowly popular nationalistic) religion, as the religion of the God of all human beings who in his commandments has given a moral law, the way of life, which holds for all. Here the focal point was transferred from rite and cult to ethics. Judaism also presented itself as a 'philosophy' which could do justice to the questions of thinking people and which emerged from venerable books as a religion of revelation with the aura of ancient wisdom. The Christian mission followed the Jewish mission in making these emphases. It seized the same chances and exploited them. Judaism, which was present all over the world and engaged in gaining recruits, provided favourable conditions for Christian mission which must not be underestimated. Not only did Christian preachers find Jewish synagogue communities already there wherever they went, in which they could canvass successfully; they also found the Jewish image of God, its ethics, its community existence, its possession of the Bible and other features. These in fact proved to be a preparation or a bridge for the Christian mission, as a result of which the Jewish mission was soon superseded.

The favourable conditions also include the religious toleration of the Roman state. The rise of a new religion like Christianity was quite possible under the Roman view of religion and the policy adopted over it, but this was on condition that citizens performed their religious obligations to the state cult (Chapter III). In principle there were no restrictions on non-Roman religions. And in the third century the world crisis which the empire experienced as a result of military and economic catastrophes and epidemics also helped it along. In the face of increasing uncertainty, Christianity had the advantage of making clear statements about the world and history, of having an assured view of salvation, a clear picture of the future, and directives for life; all this certainly attracted many people.

But there were also unfavourable conditions. These include the anti-Christian pogroms and persecutions (see III, 1, 2), which were sometimes a great hindrance to church activities. They threatened to interrupt the ongoing existence and even more the further spread of

Christianity, and of course must also have made people wary of becoming Christians; they also showed up the weakness of many Christians (who lapsed). Finally, there were many thresholds in the doctrine or theology of Christianity which pagans or Jews found it hard to get over. Much of its content was simply absurd to such people (e.g. monotheism, the incarnation of God, history as revelation, the notion of the resurrection). So Christian preaching contained a series of difficulties because it clashed with so many traditional views. The outer form of Christianity, for example the fact that (initially) it had no temple, altar or images (of gods), as pagans noted critically, told against it, because it thus lacked the characteristics of a (cultic) religion. And the exclusivist claim of Christians to the truth, which was keenly felt, could sometimes, like much else, seem very offensive. Moreover the many internal disputes and divisions, and any inadequacies in Christianity, had a negative effect.

5. Methods, preaching, motives for conversion

Here we are concerned with the practical ways, means and motives in missionary history which led to the numerous conversions to Christianity. In the first decades, itinerant Christian preachers had made mission their exclusive task and were the ones really responsible for Christian expansion. They were in fact 'specialists' in mission. According to Matt.10.9–14 we must imagine that their behaviour differed strikingly, as a result of religious inspiration. But they seem only to have existed until the third century, and after that at most only in isolated instances. This type of missionary died out, but the mission and expansion of Christianity continued nevertheless.

Recruitment to Christianity was intensive and successful in other ways. Quite evidently, in the first place it took place simply through the presence of Christians. By their clearly changed life-style, by their talk of the new faith and their community life, Christians drew public attention to themselves. The many different social contacts of everyday life proved infectious. In practice all Christians were engaged in this kind of recruitment: the mere fact that they were Christians could speak to others and convince them. Accordingly, Christianity arose wherever Christians went: as seamen, emigrants, travelling merchants; as officials, soldiers, slaves or prisoners of war. Thus in the first centuries Christianity was not a matter of preaching, 'professional missionaries' and organization (this was not the case even in earliest Christianity), but quite directly the result of the co-existence of Christians and non-Christians. Here church history is the history of mission.

This kind of recruitment extended from the lowest social levels (contacts at work places and among domestic slaves) through relations in business and so-called social life to the sphere of culture (schools, philosophy, literature). The inconspicuous and therefore uncontrollable recruitment at the 'lowest' level was particularly successful. The wooing away of the young by Christian domestic servants (house slaves) and the striking transplantation of the new superstition (as the pagans called it) among dependents gave Christianity the reputation among anxious pagans of subversion and rebellion against well-tried tradition and honourable religion and order (see e.g. Celsus, in Origen, *Contra Celsum* III, 55; Minucius Felix, *Octavius*, 8.4).

So it is impossible to talk of a programme and methods of mission in the narrower sense in the late second century. It is worth noting in connection with present notions that the early church did not have any planned initiative and organization of mission. Nothing is known of ministries or institutions specifically planned for the mission to the Gentiles or to the Jews. Accordingly, world mission was not a central theme of the theology and preaching of the early church. In earliest Christianity things had been different, but at a later date there was evidently reflection on the state of the mission to the nations and the various parts of the earth because it was believed that the end of the world was connected with the completion of the mission to the world (see above, II, 1). But in general, the view discussed above, that the apostles had engaged in mission and completed the task, was the prevalent one. So mission to the nations was not seen as still being a relevant task for the church. As a result there were also no regular and continuous planned enterprises to carry Christianity to the lands of the barbarians, near or far, or to the islands in the ocean which people knew had not yet been reached by the gospel; this activity was carried on only sporadically. Nor was there mission even to those territories of the Roman empire which had not yet been Christianized or had been Christianized only in part. It was proudly pointed out that geographically Christianity had penetrated far wider than Judaism (e.g. by Justin, *Dialogue with Trypho* 117, 1,4,5), and even further than the Romans had ever got with their conquest of the world (see e.g. Tertullian, *Adversus Judaeos* VII, 4); the basic assumption was thus that virtually the whole world had already been confronted with the gospel.

This differing view of the mission situation between earliest Christianity and the later period explains why, while earliest Christianity certainly made direct efforts at mission, as for example in the case of Paul and his missionary journeys and of course in the case of many other unknown figures, at a later date organized, deliberate mission was not carried on in the same style and no special instruments were developed for it. However, there were initiatives on the part of individual bishops towards a more planned mission, above all in the country, which on the whole had not been Christianized, and these increased in the time of Constantine (fourth century). But the 'method' still followed the style of the early mission, i.e. first gaining a foothold in all significant cities and being present throughout the world by a network of communities (though the mesh was a relatively wide one). The contours of later mission history then become evident more in the mission to the Goths, Arabs and other peoples in the fourth century by missionaries commissioned for the task. But strictly speaking the early church did not use any 'methods' in the sphere of the empire. It drew attention to itself and recruited through its alternative character in teaching, cult, fellowship and ethics, and also through its capacity for adaptation and syncretism. In all these conditions, which were more a matter of chance, a purposeful and steady mission was carried out. It was the duty of clergy and laity, and consisted in living and teaching Christianity. In the fourth century John Chrystostom wrote: 'There would be no more pagans if we were really Christians.'

The fact that by the end of the fourth century the whole population of the empire (apart from minorities) understood itself as a closed Christian society has more to do with the legislation of Christian emperors enacted in the meantime and with political pressure on pagans, and is only in part the consequence of mission. However, the success of mission preceded and laid the foundation for this new situation. Moreover with some exceptions, during the time of the imperial church the church's mission did not address itself to the Jews because they were considered a hopeless prospect.

Originally there was also explicit mission preaching in the synagogue, in streets and squares. What did it offer, where did it begin, and what did it emphasize in particular? We can read the approach and pattern of early Christian preaching to Jews in Mark 1.15; Acts 7.2–53; 13.16–41. It spoke in exclusively Jewish notions and categories. Preaching to the Gentiles, the pagans, was different. Their pagan presuppositions had to be noted; the preaching had to lead to monotheism, proclaim a new ethic, announce the coming judgment, make hearers familiar with the resurrection, and preach Christ as judge and saviour (I Thess.1.9f.; I Cor.8.4–6; Acts 26.20). In addition there were the life and death, words, miracles and passion of Jesus. This preaching stressed human anxiety and hope by describing the threatening state of present existence and offering deliverance in the form of redemption understood in Christian terms. As well as speaking of God, Jesus Christ and salvation, the preaching spoke emphatically of the moral consequences of a changed life. Initially this missionary instrument of direct preaching by missionaries played a paramount role. Then its significance declined. But there are also individual texts from later bishops on the basis of which one can reconstruct their mission preaching: it referred to the folly of paganism, then described Christianity, and removed all difficulties in the way of accepting the faith by explaining and presenting Christianity by means of pagan notions, often in a strange way. Some bishops took great pains and used much wisdom in winning over unbelievers through Christian preaching or conversion.

Thus the existence of Christianity as a church in the society of the time and the explicit instruction of people in the new faith led to conversions. The concrete motives for conversion probably differed in the case of individual recruits. Without doubt one prominent motive was that in its way Christianity met the human desire for truth, i.e. for knowledge of the actual truth about God, the world and human beings in the face of the frustration and uncertainty caused by the many offers in religions and philosophies. From the knowledge of this truth people were promised redemption, which they sought in liberation from fate and guilt, and which they found in Christianity. Freedom is one of the basic terms in early Christianity for the new existence attained in faith. Christians in late antiquity clearly experienced this freedom, for example, in the removal of the burden of fear of demons, in the penitential ritual as a removal of the burden of severe moral guilt, and gained meaning for their lives independently of the troublesome events in the history and politics of their time. A further motive was the attractive ideal of Christian holiness which people saw realized first in every baptized person, then for a long time in martyrs, and from the fourth century in monks, though in principle it was accepted that this holiness was the duty of all Christians. Repentance and reorientation followed this course. As a community of believers Christianity offered the help of a common effort and mutual reinforcement under powerful leadership (that of the bishop), with a specific creed and with clear requirements. Of course, everyone was also aware of the many kinds of social activity which the church organized, and for many people these were a reason for being interested in Christianity. Mention should be made of the particular forms of Christian worship, the liturgy, and also a possible attractiveness of the Bible because of its age and content. However, these attractive motives did not always come into play, and often they were effective only in a popularized or trivialized version. A delight in miracles, a belief in the devil, a magical understanding of the church's sacraments, the piety of martyrs, veneration of the saints and the like were another kind of motive for conversion, and certainly played a major role.

For all the success, however, from the beginning the fact of pseudo-conversions and semi-conversions was fatal to the church; the reasons for these lay in a lack of earnestness or knowledge, in weakness and a lack of understanding, and from the fourth century also in a calculation of political advantage.

Bibliography

E. M. B. Green, *Evangelism in the Early Church*, Hodder and Stoughton
    and Eerdmans 1970
Adolf von Harnack, *The Expansion of Christianity in the First Four
    Centuries*, London 1904–5 (two vols)
Martin Hengel, 'The Origins of the Christian Mission', in *Between Jesus
    and Paul*, SCM Press and Fortress Press 1983
A. D. Nock, *Conversion*, Oxford University Press 1933

III

Society, State and Christianity

The relationship between society, the state and Christianity must be seen in terms of their respective interests. Here we have the history of a co-existence which was initially difficult for Christians and then issued in open conflict at a social, political and intellectual level; finally, however, there was a mutual understanding between the state and the church as a result of a changed political assessment of Christianity by the state (emperor), and consequently society and Christianity became identical. The reason for the initial conflicts between the Roman state and Christianity is the incompatibility of the claims on both sides.

1. The period before Constantine (to 312/313 CE)

(a) The detachment and isolation of Christianity

For some time, both the state and social institutions and conditions were a matter of indifference to early Christianity; they were part of the 'world' which, with no future, was facing its end and which would be replaced by the new age. Christians were citizens of another world (Phil. 3.20; John 18.36), with no constructive interest in present conditions. However, as in Rev.17.1–6, the state could also become a demon. The position taken by Paul (Rom.13.1–7), of an unproblematical and loyal affirmation of the state, and the Christian practice of praying for the emperor, is already broader. To begin with, the relationship between Christians and the state was not a specific concern: the state took no notice of this small religious group among many others, and Christians took no notice of the state, which was part of the current bankrupt state of things facing an imminent final catastrophe, even if it was still fulfilling its functions. This situation changed only when Christians formed a numerically striking and then significantly large proportion of the population.

However, in the first three centuries Christianity created a very problematical relationship to the state and society for itself by its mode of appearance and patterns of behaviour; this arose out of Christian peculiarities and deviations and was fraught with refusals on the part of Christians to engage in some public activities. It was inevitable that one day the public would react.

The first cause was the religious difference of Christians, and the alien appearance which they presented to their contemporaries. This difference drew down on them the dangerous charge of godlessness, which meant two things: first of all it was an accusation (already made, for example, against Socrates) of having forsaken the gods of society (the polis) and thus being a disruptive factor in the stabilizing and protective order of society. Christians acknowledged this 'atheism' publicly (e.g. Justin, *Apology* I, 6, 1). Secondly, as applied to Christians the charge of atheism also meant that because of their deviant religious practice they were denied the status of a religion, since they had neither images nor temples and altars, a fact which they also acknowledged. The 'atheistic' otherness of Christianity irritated and provoked the pagans, and it isolated the Christians. The God of the Christians or worship of this God in fact distinguished them qualitatively from the pagan understanding of cult and religion.

See Minucius Felix, *Octavius* 32.1; Origen, *Contra Celsum* VII, 62, 2f. They did not have the divine images, sacrifices and ceremonies which went with pagan religions, from which we can conclude what the community will have looked like at that time: with the service of the word of God and the eucharistic meal as liturgy, with the forms of life in the community and everything else, early Christianity did not seem to be recognizable to contemporaries as a religion or cultic association in the usual sense. The vividness of this difference did not diminish when in the course of time the church provided itself with images, temples and altars and explicitly celebrated the eucharist as a cultic sacrifice with priests.

A further difference was no less problematical. With their biblical monotheism, Christians clashed with a pagan concept of divinity which had a very different religious stamp. Certainly the notion of a dominant god was known in the pantheon of Roman polytheism, but the other gods existed nevertheless. And the Roman view was that they had the historical and politically relevant function of being national deities; in other words, they were responsible for the government and the protection of the peoples assigned to them. The religious and political ordering of the world was based on this. With their absolute monotheism, Christians put this view of the world in question and thus ran counter to fundamental notions of order. The pagan critic Celsus (end of the second century) objected to Matt.6.24 ('no one can serve two masters') and to the political application of this maxim by Christians to God and gods: 'This is the language of the rebellion (*stasis*) of people who cut themselves off and detach themselves from others' (Origen, *Contra Celsum* VIII, 2).

So the Christian belief in God was politically dangerous, and it distanced Christians considerably from society. Pagan objections arose out of a concern for religion, humanity and culture. Pagans saw Christians as advocating a monotheism which they felt to be wrong and pernicious because it broke up traditional, proven religion. Christians therefore represented a danger to society. The heaven of gods, which justified the multiplicity of nations under Roman rule as the world order of divine providence, had to be recognized by all citizens; but Christians recognized only the one God of creation and history as the guarantor of human salvation and the future of the nations. Because their religous conviction and praxis differed, they became outsiders, and when it came to the worst they were even seen as disloyal opponents to the established political and religious order. Thus on occasion they drew aggression upon themselves as enemies of religion or the gods.

The theological and religious distance described above, with its political implications, meant that Christians were socially isolated. Because of their divergent views, they had to go their own way in many spheres of public life where these were related to religion and the cult. For example, Christians avoided or repudiated the many popular festivals and the rich customs based on long traditions rooted in the people, in other words central elements of the socialization of a society; at any rate, Christians did not take part in them because they all had a religious and cultic origin, quality and meaning and were therefore incompatible with Christian life. This also applied to plays in the theatre and games in the circus, which played a major social role for the public and the individual, as religious and social events or as leisure-time attractions.

Thus Christians distanced themselves from the focal points of social life and spheres of interest. The pagans must have seen this evidence that Christians were religious and social outsiders confirmed by the fact that in addition they led a strange religious life of their own in their communities, a life which sometimes even seemed scandalous. As the Christian gatherings did not take place publicly, and sometimes were held at night, all kinds of derogatory hypotheses and criticisms were bandied about by the pagans, and slanders and malicious caricatures and distortions were also disseminated. The sometimes grotesque and coarse criticisms of Christianity were based on misunderstandings and arose from popular aggression against an unpopular minority.

As a result of such aversion, Christianity was forced into isolation by outside pressures; however, without doubt it also contributed towards fortifying this isolation both by the limits it set itself and by its own (church) organization and the rhythm of community life with its own cultic festivals, practices and customs. One important consequence of this was that at an early stage Christianity developed an almost exclusively defensive ethic of detachment from the world which it continued to maintain later, even when its relationship to the 'world' had fundamentally changed.

Christians increased their detachment from the non-Christian environment by other features in their activity and the impression that they made. There was much that proved provocative. Where Christians were engaged in seeking converts, a regular ploy took the form of a devastating critique of paganism or a proof of the superiority of Christianity to paganism. Both sounded offensive to pagan ears. The claim that a Christianity which had only just appeared on the scene was in sole possesion of the truth and that its ethics were universally valid must have seemed abhorrently arrogant, especially as the surrounding world hardly knew any claims of this exclusive kind. The zeal for conversion was thought to be importunate; the consciousness of election put on display to be grotesque. Moreover Christians were criticized for not being interested in the concerns of the state and society. Christian missionary success also contributed to the widespread unpopularity of the Christians, because it split marriages and families and led many people to apostatize from the well-tried pious traditions of their ancestors. Provocative in its behaviour, but in substance a primitive superstition and in its social consequences the ruin of the empire – that was the widespread image of Christianity where people came to grips with it critically. Christians declared worthless all the values prized by society – science, education, culture, possessions, career (though here their principles were often more rigorous than their practice); they took a sceptical view of oaths, official positions and reputations.

Because of the declared lack of interest on the part of Christians in public affairs, in addition to these charges they were understandably also accused of enjoying the benefits of society without sharing its political burdens. This related especially to the sore point of military service. Up to the end of the second century, though later in a diminished or only isolated way, Christians condemned military service and refused to engage in it (though at that time there was no general conscription), for moral reasons (murder, power, brutality) and with cultic objections (the oath taken on the standard, sacrifices). This self-dispensation of Christians from some of the key obligations of society was particularly striking and incurred corresponding criticism.

However, Christians defended themselves against the many objections they met with yet more arguments, understanding all hostility in religious terms as the resistance of unbelieving error and the enemies of God. In particular they energetically disputed the charge that as citizens they were useless, uninvolved, unreliable, destructive and thus dangerous. They constantly asserted their respect for the emperor and their interest in the public good. Above all, they referred to their prayer to the only true and helpful God, which would bring more blessing to humankind and the empire than the whole pagan cult. So in the first three centuries the relationship of Christians to the state was that of a fundamental loyalty, with strict reservations about the cultic claims of emperor and empire.

However, the distance described above, which without doubt came close to confrontation, is not all that has to be said about the relationship of the early church to state and society. Much could be said about an unproblematical agreement between Christians and the society of late antiquity. For example, the impact made by the charitable practices of the early church on its pagan environment is worth mentioning. Here too the Christians were untypical and deviants, but here as a rule the pagan reaction was positive, and only sometimes ironical or slanderous. Pagans probably felt the lack of social obligations which Christians took seriously under the demand to love their neighbours to be a defect in their own religion; at any rate they regarded the charitable activity of Christians as being to their credit. Moreover the contemporary mission successes of Christianity show that many pagans did not criticize the otherness of Christianity polemically, but accepted it as an alternative to their own way of life.

But time and again there were situations in which objections from the side of state politicians, religious criticism or popular aversion proved decisive and led to anti-Christian measures. Christianity for its part criticized pagan religion, complained about unjustified reprisals and, unabashed, offered its own new faith as a way.

(b) Polemic and persecution

So pagans could criticize a series of aspects of Christianity. From the time of earliest Christianity down to the fourth century there is evidence of widespread active repudiation of Christianity among the population. Society saw itself increasingly led to oppose the spread of this new religion in the interest of its 'world view'. The resistance was offered on different levels. In addition to the numerous prejudices and attacks of a popular kind from the second century on, there was philosophical polemic at a high level, a few examples of which are known. The most important names among such critics of Christianity are Celsus (end of the second century), Porphyry (234–304) and the emperor Julian (331–363; emperor 361–363). These were men with a philosophical education, who out of a concern for the ongoing existence of venerable religion and a humane intellectual culture in a society which derived from ancient tradition analysed Christianity as an unfounded superstition which scorned all reason, and passionately attacked it as a dangerous, misleading, destructive innovation. Their criticism was based on a relatively accurate and pertinent knowledge of Christianity, especially the Bible, and they formulated clever objections which the average Christian could not cope with. Because of its motivation, the criticism was presented with philosophical and religious commitment, but at the same time it was markedly polemical (as were the Christian responses).

So Christianity was ruled out of court for discussion by the philosophers for a number of reasons. First of all, this criticism pointed out, the truth is not something very recent in history, but venerable tradition. How was it that Christianity came so late if it brings the decisive truth for all men? Furthermore, its alleged truth comes from an uneducated man (Jesus) with followers (the apostles) who were no wiser. The teachers of the Christians were utterly incompetent, unserious people. No wonder that they have the most banal notion of God, the soul, the other world and so on, and draw their followers from the lowly, uneducated strata of the population. Truth can only be attained and communicated through the critical efforts of a small elite (the philosophers); it does not drop into one's lap (through an alleged revelation). Furthermore Christianity is not original and new, as Christians claim, but has been taken over from the Jews. Its utter inadequacy is also evident from the thinness of its holy scriptures and the absence of any rational basis and explanation for its controversial themes. Christianity calls for (blind) faith and has no foundation for its belief. The importance of miracle in the case of Jesus and Christianity underlines its generally barbaric and proletarian character, since (as magic) it satisfies the wishes of the mob.

Thus right from the start Christianity was dismissed in a contemptuous and scathing way. However, the objections which pointed out how philosophically unthinkable biblical Christian statements were proved to be more serious. For example it was claimed to be quite impossible that God should have come in a mortal body, i.e. should have experienced change. Because of its humiliations, failures and platitudes the life of Jesus, understood as a revelation or epiphany of the divine, was thought perverse and ridiculous, and a Son of God on the cross was quite impossible. In principle these objections were directed against the biblical idea of a

God who acts, makes decisions, shows emotions (love, repentance, hatred): in other words – philosophically speaking – is subject to change. The pagan thinker regarded the fact of the resurrection not only as an invention but also as not even desirable: he did not want to be redeemed *with* the body but *from* the body – a different anthropology. It was the same with the picture of the world: the biblical Christian notion that human beings are the centre of the world and its most precious element, and that the cosmos is there for their sake, was deemed overweening arrogance. On the contrary, human beings were hidden in the greater reality of the cosmos.

Greek philosophical thought looked on almost all the fundamental categories, ideas and hopes in a different way from Christianity. The perspectives of the religious difference described in the previous section belong in this connection. Here again the political and social damage which pagans saw arising from the aberrations and propaganda of Christianity play their part in giving the criticism its edge, its acuteness and its focus: educated pagans dealt with Christianity, that phenomenon which was beyond discussing, carefully and in detail because it seemed that people could be led astray by such nonsense. The critics warned and cajoled, and hoped that those who had gone over to Christianity would again reflect on the fact that they belonged to the world of the old religion and culture (for the Christian answer see Chapter VII).

The persecutions of Christians in the Roman empire have their causes in the sum of the points of conflict described above. Certainly the first persecutions came from the Jews (see Chapter I, 3 and 4) and there were special reasons for them: the synagogue resorted to sanctions against part of the earliest community for blasphemy and heresy (Acts 6.8–8.3; 26.11; cf. 12.4; Josephus, *Antiquities* XX, 200); and during the Second Jewish War against the Romans (132–135 CE) there was a bloody persecution of Christians by the rebels in Palestine, evidently because they did not support the rebellion and were regarded as collaborators. We must also reckon with the same thing during the First Jewish War (66–70 CE). But the so-called Roman persecutions were much more long-lasting and serious. As a process and a fate they left deep marks on the theology and spirituality of early Christianity and its understanding of the world and history. Accounts of martyrdoms, theological writings and the history of spirituality attest the intensive preoccupation of the early church with this theme.

In noting the dates and courses of 'persecutions of Christians' it is important to note that the term usually denotes two different processes, which are not identical, namely the official state measures against Christians (those of the emperors), which were ordered and directed centrally, and the numerous spontanous pogroms, i.e. attacks by the population. The two must be considered separately. Pogroms made up the majority of the persecutions, while there were official state actions against the Christians only from the middle of the third century to the beginning of the fourth.

The first known use of violence against Christians, by the emperor Nero (54–68) in 64, was not for religious reasons and to this extent was not a persecution of Christians in the narrower sense. At that time, probably to quieten down public indignation at the burning of Rome, for which he himself had been responsible, Nero looked for a sufficiently unpopular group as a scapegoat, so that he could inflict cruel punishment on them as a diversion without arousing any public sympathy. He could even expect applause from the population for his brutal attack on the Christians. This is characteristic of the image which people had of them at so early a date. Peter and Paul may have been killed at that time.

Apparently Christians were also executed under the emperor Domitian (81–96), who instigated compulsory emperor worship of his person and undertook political 'cleansings' of the usual kind; here the religious criterion of loyalty, performance of the cult, may have played a role. We do not know more.

There were then numerous persecutions in the course of the second and third centuries. Clearly these were limited locally and instigated from below. Only after attacks and denunciations from the people did the authorities occasionally intervene. In the trials which then ensued there was a chronic legal uncertainty about what Christians were really to be punished for (which was usually unspoken). Were Christians to be attacked as such and in every instance because to be a Christian was criminal in itself, or was being a Christian in itself innocuous, and had criminal acts first to be demonstrated in each individual case? The publication of the correspondence between a governor, Pliny, in Asia Minor and the

emperor Trajan (98–117) on this issue (c. 112 CE) evidently led in
the subsequent period to a dubious legal practice: the state did not
itself punish Christians, but legal penalties were imposed on the
basis of private accusations if the accused did not obey the court's
demand to desist from Christianity. Although evidence to the
contrary was produced in hearings, being a Christian was thus
generally assumed to be criminal. At least the criminal condition of
resistance and stubbornness against the authorities was construed
from persistence in Christianity, which seemed rebellious. However, the background to this criminalization was the hostility to
society which was attributed to the Christians. Despite a degree of
legal protection for Christians against anonymous and false accusations provided by the emperor Hadrian (117–138), this situation
was permanently threatening for them and made possible the
condemnations of Christians on the basis of popular accusations, of
which there is evidence for various parts of the empire. These
persecutions were local, often fortuitous, and usually did not last
long.

Systematic oppressive measures by the state (as attempts to
eliminate Christians) began only in the third century, but they were
of an unprecedented harshness. The threatening crises of this
century (economic and financial, along with military defeats and
epidemics) required the state to take effective measures towards
consolidation. These included a conservative religious policy which
took the form of a concern for the cult in order to ensure divine help.
In 250 the emperor Decius (249–251) ordered universal compulsory
sacrifice on pain of death; though this applied to all inhabitants of the
empire, it was clear that it was meant particularly to affect the
Christians, whose numbers had meanwhile increased. The aim was
the annihilation of Christianity, not of the Christians. By demon-
strating their loyalty in the cult they were to be restored to the
religion and tradition of the empire. Refusal inexorably led to the
imposition of the penalty. At that time the church suffered severe
losses. It had many martyrs, but even more apostates. Subsequently
Valerian (253–260) and Gallienus (253–268) also pursued policies
of persecution, but as early as 260 Gallienus already enacted an edict
of tolerance and thus put a halt to this policy. The more immediate
reason for the emperors' political concern with Christians at this

time was the manifest increase of this politically suspect minority in the third century (see Chapter II), which moreover was taking place in a period of growing problems for politics and the economy. The solidarity and loyalty of citizens and the favour of the gods was thus more important than ever. All this also had an effect on the policy of Diocletian (284–305), the harshness of which was catastrophic for Christians. The repression carried through from 303 onwards, methodically planned and implemented by stages (first against the clergy, then also against the laity), was again clearly aimed at the annihilation of Christianity and at restoring Christians to a better insight. In the case of Diocletian, as with his predecessors, these measures are to be seen within the framework of a comprehensive policy of reform and restoration. However, the clearest evidence that the expected success did not materialize is the edict of tolerance issued by Galerius (305–311), initially co-emperor with and then successor to Diocletian, and a declared enemy of Christians. Though a persecutor, he issued his edict on 30 April 311 and shortly before his death declared that the policy of persecution had come to an end. In so doing he acknowledged its failure; almost more important, however, is the fact that he invited Christians 'to pray to *their* God for our salvation (*salus*, i.e. of the emperor), for that of the state and for their own'. This is the first time in the history of Christianity and the Roman empire that the power and help of the Christian God is officially taken into account in the political 'guidelines' of a pagan emperor, thus acknowledging a positive contribution of Christians to politics (through prayer or the cult). The edict of Galerius meant that there could now be Christians, but 'on condition that they do not act against the state constitution in any way'. Here the requirement of loyalty was fictitiously being renewed once again at the very moment when it had been given up because it had failed: Christians could not fufil the demands of the pagan state in the cultic sphere. That being so, according to Galerius, at least the empire should benefit from the Christian cult. This was a turning point in the relationship between the Roman empire and Christianity.

After this edict of Galerius, despite the declaration of tolerance in the Milan protocol (313) by Constantine and Licinius, there were further persecutions in the East under Constantine's co-emperors or anti-emperors (Maximinus Daia, Licinius) until Constantine became sole ruler in 324. They affected Christians as potential supporters of the rival Constantine, so that their motive was tactical rather than religious, but they were carried through with religious ideology.

Generally speaking, all state persecutions were relatively inconsistent and were not carried through uniformly. As a result their effectiveness was limited. In the West of the empire they were less consistent and harsh than in the East. When Galerius enacted his edict of tolerance in 311, persecutions of Christians as a political means had long been contrary to views and practices in the West. Moreover there were long periods without persecution, which were even predominant, though they were often not without danger. But of course the process was a severe test for the church, and ultimately came to grief in the face of its power of resistance. Being so constantly under the threat of martyrdom, the church became able to face persecution with increasing strength. The 'penalties' imposed on communities consisted in the arrest of their leaders, the confiscation of cemeteries and buildings, and the seizure of cultic writings (Bible, etc.) and vessels; in the case of individuals they consisted in arrest, restrictions, confiscation of possessions and removal of rights, banishment, forced labour, torture and mutilation, and in extreme cases execution. But there were not only state penal measures but also pogroms with uncontrolled brutality.

The two sides saw the grounds for the persecutions very differently. The church saw the real cause as being the godlessness and moral turpitude of the persecutors, who were thought to be possessed by the devil, raging against the servants of the true God, or as being God's punishment for the bad state of the churches. So there were purely religious aspects. However, on the part of the state and society the decisive factor was the whole syndrome of rational and emotional barriers listed above, which stood between Christianity and the surrounding world and in which the political aspects were decisive. The issue was the loyalty of Christians and their agreement with everyone else on a religious and political world view. The Roman approach was fundamentally to see everything, and religion first and foremost, from a political perspective. In the case of alien religions, any assessment and decision was always dependent on the political situation at home or abroad (public order and security, reasons of state). Because such considerations often had only temporary significance and could change rapidly, the Roman religious policy against alien cults was often as variable and inconsistent as it was in its treatment of Christianity. There were further reasons for this: the Romans were convinced that they also had an obligation to alien gods; moreover as 'world conquerors' they sought to practise the political virtues of generosity, mildness and tolerance in connection with alien peoples, their customs and their religions. So these different considerations could lead to a highly inconsistent policy fluctuating between persecution and tolerance.

In addition to the political side, the whole business also had a legal side. We need to investigate the legal basis for the measures against Christianity. There was no general law against non-Roman cults in the empire. A foreign religion was no crime for the Romans. But they were clear about the value of the worship of the gods, ancestral customs and the authority of the state. Where these foundations seemed under threat, no special law was needed for counter-measures to be taken; they were enough as guidelines for political action. Only during the third century and at the beginning of the fourth did the state enact laws (edicts) against Christianity. Up till then the general right of the authorities to impose punishment to maintain public order (*coercitio*) was sufficient. However, without precise laws there was always room for debate as to whether an alien religion was punishable under law or not. Hence the legal un-certainty over Christians in the second century, mentioned above. In cases of doubt, however, things went against the Christians, because as a result of the many negative prejudices the doubt tended to become condemnation. When from Decius onwards relevant laws then imposed penalties on being a Christian, the legal situation became clear; and these laws had to be repealed by edicts of tolerance if the situation was to change.

We know of hardly any assessments of these developments by pagans. By contrast, a series of reactions within Christianity are important, some of which were a presupposition for the survival of Christianity, and others a consequence of this. It was of decisive significance that in their distress Christians not only maintained the universal virtues of loyalty, steadfastness, contempt for death and so on but with their new faith had quite singular possibilities for rising above the situation and finding comfort in it: the tortured, executed and risen Jesus, the ideal of a discipleship which shared his fate in suffering violent death on the way to life, and their own tangible similarity with him in suffering (in the passion) – all this immediately gave meaning to cruel events. Jesus' forecasts of persecution in the Gospels (Mark 13.9–13; Matt.10.16–25), the conscious expectation of the woes marking the end of the world, the idea of the dramatic battle between truth and error, meant that no panic developed: things *had to* be like this. Of course, not all were heroes of faith, but these sources provided an explanation of events for the community and the individual. In the elite of martyrs as christlike figures the whole community found the realization of their ideal and thus their identity, even if not everyone achieved this ideal. Practical community theology took on corresponding features in ethics and piety. Moreover the pressure from outside reinforced the cohesion of the community and accelerated the development of a fixed organization (see Chapter IV, 2); through the problems which arose, it furthered communication between the churches at the synods which proved to be necessary. Reactions to persecution also included self-defence against unjust charges and measures. In individual cases this self-defence even intensified to the point of open aggression against persecutors.

Mention was made above, in connection with the reactions of Christians to persecutions, of the effects of these events on the spirituality, theology and solidarity of the community. The harsh trials and the fact of the apostasy of many of its members (especially under Decius) made the community's discipline stricter, in order to avoid such things. Faith, morality and an ascetic attitude prepared individuals for an emergency. In these difficult conditions, the office and person of bishop became increasingly significant in the task of the spiritual and administrative leadership of often unsettled communities (see Chapter IV, 2, a). Episcopal authority grew, in particular in connection with a dramatic conflict in the early church, namely that over penitence. A decision had to be made within a short space of time as to whether it was possible to grant the urgent wish of many Christians who had weakened in the Decian persecution to be received back into the church, in other words whether there was a possibility for them to repent. Their chance of salvation was at stake here. Opinions on this among church leaders extended from the tolerance of the 'confessors' (those Christians who had confessed their faith in persecution despite threats and as a result were perhaps imprisoned and maltreated), who received back the lapsed without further ado by virtue of their own perfection, to the rigorist position, according to which the only possibility for these unfortunates was for the church to leave them to the judgment of God. The discussion broadened into a dispute over ideal and compromise in Christianity; it was principally carried on between Bishop Cyprian (died 258) in Carthage and the Roman church. Cyprian, whose theology and practice was of great significance for the development of the episcopate in the West generally, won the day (not only in North Africa) with the proposal that a return to the church could be possible for the fallen in a regulated and very strict penitential process which lay solely in the hands of the bishop, who had been endowed with the relevant authority by God. In protest, the opposition movement formed a separate rigorist church of the 'pure' (*katharoi*), excluding all sinners. Its leader was the Roman presbyter Novatian. This schism lasted for centuries, and the Novatian church (Novatianism) existed throughout the empire. This, too, was a consequence of the persecutions, as was another great schism which developed in North Africa in 307 (or 311/12). Following the line of strict African church discipline, some bishops, including a certain Donatus, held the consecration of Bishop Caecilian in Carthage to be invalid because there had been a so-called *traditor codicum* among the consecrating bishops, namely a bishop who had weakened in persecution and had handed over sacred writings or vessels to the authorities. The dogmatic issue was the dependence of the validity and effectiveness of a sacrament on the moral quality of the one bestowing it. The church split again over this dispute: alongside the catholic church the Donatist church (Donatism) came into being; in Augustine's day (fourth/fifth century) it was still the larger of the two (see also Chapters III, 2, d and V).

The two controversies over Novatianism and Donatism brought enduring clarification to both theology and church practice. Novatian rigorism was opposed by a conviction that the bishop had authority in matters of penance in the church and by the merciful attitude of the community; but the tolerance of the confessors was thought to trivialize sin (apostasy). Against the Donatist objections the church maintained that the sacrament is independent of the one who administers it, which protects the recipient from an intolerable insecurity. The two schisms cost the church much effort, substance and credibility. They belong to the history of the confrontation between church and state as consequences of the persecution of Christians.

2. *The changed situation after Constantine*

After the failure of repeated measures by a number of emperors to do away with Christianity, with the edict of tolerance proclaimed by Galerius in 311 in the name of all four emperors ruling at the time (Galerius, Maximinus Daia, Constantine and Licinius) a political change of course came about within a few years. The official toleration of Christianity by Galerius, the persecuting emperor, became full recognition, equal status and promotion of Christianity under Constantine (306–337), and then at the end of the fourth century led to Christianity having an exclusive position as the imperial church and state religion (Theodosius I, 379–395); its developed structures are shown by the sixth century (Justinian I, 527–565). This process was prescribed and directed by state politics and religious legislation between the fourth and the sixth centuries. The circumstances of the church were considerably changed, and this had far-reaching consequences.

(a) *Constantine's encouragement of Christianity*

From 306 onwards Constantine (306–337) was emperor of some parts of the Western empire (Gaul and Britain). All his life he saw the decisive breakthrough of his career as being the victory over his rival in the West, Maxentius, in 312 at the so-called Milvian Bridge before Rome; for him this meant rule over the whole of the West, including Rome. Very much in keeping with his Roman understanding of religion and in the style of contemporary political propaganda, he represented this military and political success as the direct intervention of the deity, who had chosen him as its instrument and representative in the governance of the world. The people also readily saw the events as a sign of heaven's favour towards Constantine. Shortly before the decisive battle, Constantine had evidently determined to pursue a pro-Christian course in religious policy should he be successful. When he had gained the victory which was decisive for his rule in the West, despite initially unfavourable circumstances, he attributed it to his use of Christian symbols (sun and cross) as military standards and his vow to pursue a pro-Christian course. Immediately afterwards he gave indications of this new course by, for example, replacing the names of the Roman gods in official speeches or declarations with abstract terms ('deity'/*divinitas*), ceasing to perform obligatory rites of the pagan cult (sacrifice after victory) and having coins minted with the labarum (a sign consisting of the Greek letters *chi* and *rho*) on them. This change of religious policy came as a surprise to his subjects, both pagans and Christians. Granted, in the course of politics a particular cult of a particular god might often be promoted vigorously by the emperor. Constantine had not made a new kind of policy but in principle was formally continuing the policy of Diocletian in matters of constitution, administration, defence and also religion. The significance of his policy for church history and history generally lies in his choice of Christianity, which had far-reaching consequences. And he indefatigably declared to the people that his rise to power was the dawn of a new era, as other emperors had also done for their rule. Moreover in his propaganda he illustrated his own religious and political decision for Christianity in the form of a vision that he had had before the battle against Maxentius.

Other emperors (e.g. Diocletian and Licinius) also regarded such visions as a hint from the deity, and in early years Constantine himself already claimed to have had a vision of the sun god Apollo in Gaul (*Panegyrici latini* VII, 21.4f.). For people of late antiquity important decisions and decisive events were associated with miraculous signs and dreams. Constantine's vision in 312, in which his victory over Maxentius and thus his future role was announced, has come down to us in very different versions

(Lactantius, *De mortibus persecutorum* 44.5; Eusebius, *Vita Constantini* I, 26–29), but they agree on the fact that Constantine saw the sign of the cross or a Christian sign, as a result of which he allied his political career with Christianity from 312 on.

Even now, different assessments are made of Constantine, and in particular these events at the beginning of his career are disputed. The Christians, who experienced a rapid improvement in their fortunes, were convinced that the pagan ruler had been converted from idols to the Christian God by divine providence and that he was now serving to establish the truth of the gospel in the world and in history, putting an end to all repressions of Christianity. However, historically things look rather different. Constantine did not experience any conversion; there are no signs of a change of faith in him. He never said of himself that he had turned to another god. Rather, long before his decision for Christianity, in his religious attitude the emperor had quite clearly and increasingly been tending towards henothesism, which he practised in the cult of a god described with very abstract attributes. At the time when he turned to Christianity, for him this was *Sol Invictus* (the victorious sun god) in the guise of whom he had himself depicted on coins. And according to Eusebius (*Vita Constantini* I, 28), in his vision the sun (the sun god) was combined with the cross.

Constantine did not forsake this god Sol. The spectacular shift consisted in the fact that he *changed* the *cult* (the form of worship) of this god and that he chose Christianity for this cult. For him, the God of the Christians was identical with the god whom he himself worshipped. From Constantine's perspective the state needed a religion which was strictly monarchical in its view of God and the world, and which was represented and continued on earth in the political monarchy of the absolutist emperor. In his picture of the religious and political order a single (supreme) God ruled the world. The instrument of his rule on earth was the one and only emperor (Constantine would go on to establish himself in this role in the face of his rivals), who ruled the (Roman) world empire. Constantine made his choice in accordance with these criteria when he gave preference to Christianity with its exclusively sole God over the old religions of the many gods. The alternative so often posed, whether

Constantine 'became a Christian' through calculating political or honest religious motives, is thus a false one, since in Roman terms it was impossible to separate reasons of state and religion. Constantine saw Christianity through Roman eyes as a cult religion (only later did he come to understand the significance of the creed in Christianity) with recognizable structures (a hierarchical organization, an ideal unity throughout the empire, universalism, a capacity to establish itself in history) which was admirably suited to contribute to the task of the state.

In 313 Constantine and his co-emperor Licinius came to an agreement over religious policy along these lines in Milan. This Milan Protocol of 313 was promulgated to the people of the empire. It put Christianity on a par with existing cults. Later, Constantine used military force to remove Licinius as a rival in the East, and from 324 was sole ruler. As a result of this, his change of course was prepared for throughout the empire and could be consolidated. But in his religious policy Constantine was patient and tolerant; in other words, there was no hasty use of force against pagans who held the old beliefs or against Jews. However, he constantly promoted the Christianization of the empire and society through legislation, the building of churches, church policy and propaganda. In many respects his own piety remained essentially Roman and political, but it gradually took on Christian elements; however, it did not lead the emperor to seek baptism. Constantine received baptism only immediately before his death. In the role of 'bishop (overseer) of those outside' (i.e. of both Christians and non-Christians), as he evidently termed himself, in his religious practice and in politics he took heed of the Gentiles whose emperor he also was, but like every Roman emperor he supervised the cult, and that now meant Christianity.

The church found this religious policy very much to its advantage and indeed welcomed it. Now it, too, received subventions and privileges like the pagan cults. Its bishops were appointed to an elevated social status with important state roles (they were judges in the courts). Christianity enjoyed imperial protection. There were only isolated objections and criticisms, and these related only to the negative consequences of the new role of Christianity. Bishop Eusebius of Caesarea (who died around 339) is the type of churchman who was enthusiastic about the new circumstances, and he described this surprising turn of events in his writings with great optimism, from the Christian side too, as God's direction of history.

(b) The development towards the imperial church

Whereas Constantine himself did not act in a totalitarian manner, but gave Christianity and paganism equal political status (though he now sharply repudiated paganism, both subjectively and in his statements), subsequent emperors sought more vigorously to promote the church and give it privileges, while on the other hand subjecting it more to political control. Of Constantine's sons it was mainly Constantius II (337–361), and after him other fourth-century emperors, who made advances in both directions by intolerant policies and legislation. Paganism came increasingly under pressure, and possibilities for Jews were limited. By contrast the church was increasingly integrated into the state system, and this meant that it lost independence and freedom and similarly suffered massive repression from the state. Finally, heretics were treated with particular harshness as the primary disruptive factors in the new system.

We now turn to the provisional climax of this development in the fourth century. Under the emperor Theodosius I (379–395), Christianity as the imperial church was actually given the role of state religion. In an edict of 28 February 380 the emperor obligated all subjects in the empire to become Christians (thus banning paganism) according (it was said) to the faith of bishops Damasus of Rome and Peter of Alexandria, which meant the creed of the Council of Nicaea in 325 (see Chapter VIII, 3). Along with this measure went a consistent policy of imperial direction of the church without consultation with the bishops or synods. Thus the state gave Christianity the function that the cult had always had in the Roman empire, namely that of safeguarding the necessary divine worship and integrating the population in religion. Moreover the emperor made the decisions about this state religion, for which according to Roman tradition he was responsible, in his own right, by imposing a specific creed on Christianity at the very time when dogma was very confused; he stated authoritatively in the heresy law of 381 that opposition to this creed was heresy.

Such developments followed from the new role of the church as state religion. The status of Christianity as the imperial church rested on a consensus between state and church which was not without its conflicts. The reign of the emperor Justinian I (527–565) showed the symptoms once again with particular clarity. As monarch, Justinian was aware that he was the one primarily responsible for empire and religion. Politics, administration and theology were simply different spheres of the one responsibility. So he waged war to restore a disintegrating empire, but to the same end persecuted heretics, Jews, alien religions and pagans with laws (it was Justinian who closed the pagan university of Athens in 529), wrote dogmatic tractates and (like his predecessors since Constantine) summoned councils. Here Christianity as a religion was totally integrated into the functions of the state system. Already with Constantine there was a specific legal basis for this: with its ordering of the empire, Roman law also applied quite centrally to worship and priests of religion, and therefore now also to Christian priests. Thus the church was part of the Roman legal system and subject to the legislator (the emperor) as part of the structure of public order. In its new character as a corporation (*corpus*) in the legal sense, however, the church also had a title in law, on the basis of which the emperor could make subventions, gifts and the like to it.

(c) The Christian emperor and the pagans

We must assume that numerically Christians were still clearly in the minority at the time of Constantine. However, this will soon have changed because of the new religious policy. Still, the Christian emperors' idea of a rapid unification of the empire under the Christian creed was not easy to carry through, because a quite considerable part of the population at all levels remained pagan or indifferent. People held fast to the old traditions in a conservative way. The criticism of Christianity from the time before Constantine continued even now in the changed circumstances. The pagans saw the shift under Constantine as a political disaster amounting to the loss of all divine support. In the person of the emperor Julian (361–363) this conservative reaction for the moment even became a political force once again. Julian reduced and criticized Christianity, and attempted to revive pagan religion with deliberate incentives and to make it attractive (among other things as a rival to the Christian form of church life). This was only a brief episode, but the pagan opposition continued. The longer the new state of things lasted, the more strongly this opposition consolidated in a fanatical and reactionary persistence in passive and sometimes even active resistance. One famous instance is the dispute over the altar of Victory, an expression of the old faith of the Roman senatorial aristocracy. In 382 the emperor Gratian (367–383) removed from the senate hall in Rome the altar which since 29 BCE had stood there before the statue of the goddess of Victory, and on which sacrifices were offered before sessions. Of course it was a prestigious religious object of the first order. Constantine had already caused it to be removed in 356, but Julian restored it. In the years 382 and 384 senatorial circles almost managed to persuade the emperor to rescind the order by petitions, proposals and other means, but Bishop Damasus of Rome and the even more effective Bishop Ambrose of Milan made clear to the emperor where his duty to the true religion lay as ruler. The altar was never restored. From now on the pagans had permanently to cope with the intolerant gestures of the new religion.

A further sign of the separation of the Roman emperor from the old cult, which must have been quite unmistakable to contemporaries, was the rejection of the imperial title *Pontifex maximus* (supreme priest) by Theodosius I in 379 and by Gratian in 382. Granted, *de facto* the emperors had long occupied the old political religious position on their own terms (which is why their predecessors since Constantine had seen no occasion to give up the title), but they had no longer been involved in the old cult.

With Constantine's sons, legislative measures by the state also began: the prohibition of pagan sacrifices and the veneration of images, the closing of temples, a halt to state subventions for the priesthoods and other acts of repression which had previously been practised against Christians. Not all emperors pursued this policy. Political calculation made the choice of means vary (as earlier with the Christians) between pressure and tolerance. In general the imperial laws were more used as a threat than actually applied. Practical politics had to be pursued with great care. However, this did not alter the fact that the imperial policy was basically intolerant. There are many examples of the church and Christians encouraging the state in this intolerance, and even of them adopting an anti-pagan attitude themselves, resorting to acts of violence against those of other beliefs and being incapable of exercising that tolerance for which they had often pleaded in the period before Constantine, when they were the ones who were suffering. As a result of the novel topicality of the question of dogmatic truth which Christianity introduced into the society of late antiquity, the other, more problematical, side which began to develop was a history of permanent religious intolerance.

(d) The Christian emperor and the church

As a result of the new situation of an imperial church the relationship between church and state became a problem in a hitherto unprecedented way. It had to be clarified through complicated processes or in various ways tolerated as a conflict. For the Christian emperors acted on the basis of an idea of the emperor which came down unchanged from ancient political philosophy and was decked out with basic religious concepts which did not derive from Christianity. There were inevitably collisions. The emperors and their administration had to endure at least as many costly conflicts with the church as with the pagans, Jews and heretics. And for its part the church often had great difficulty in preserving freedom from the state to regulate its own sphere of life. The state and the church had different interests in the realms of dogma and church unity. For the church, dogma had priority; for the state, religious and political unity. Moreover there was no theory on the Christian side to describe the singular position of the emperor in or over against the church: he was neither bishop nor pope, and yet he had a competence (in principle recognized by all) which in some respects went beyond that of the bishops. Furthermore Christianity had no formula of its own, no theory for its relationship to the state or for the relationship between what would later be called the two 'powers', the spiritual power of the bishops and the secular power of the state. And that was so complicated in the fourth century because – in good Roman fashion – competence was also claimed for the emperor in the sphere of religion and the cult, while in the Christian under-standing this fell only to the bishop. None of this was really clarified in the period of the early church. And views on the question differed widely, even among Christians, who were influenced by their particular church, their party or their theology. There were some developments in which new difficulties emerged for the state in late antiquity.

Thus very soon after his change of course Constantine experi-enced a first disillusionment with Christianity in the form of the Donatist dispute (see Chapters III, 1, a above and V). The church, to which he had entrusted the power of bringing unity to the empire, had itself split and was incapable of restoring its unity. In the imperial church a problem of this kind unavoidably became a political issue, since because of the superior postulate of political unity and order the emperor had to be involved in it. The Donatist dispute was on the one hand about the religious ideal of holiness and church discipline and on the other about dogmatic positions. Had Caecilian of Carthage been regularly and validly consecrated bishop in 311/312 if it was true that he had been consecrated by a *traditor*, i.e. a bishop who had weakened under persecution? Or was it necessary to recognize his rival (Majorinus, to be succeeded by Donatus), who had been appointed anti-bishop by the rigorist party in an unassailable election? The dispute was further hardened by political, social, religious and ethnic complications in North Africa, and as a schism with two separate churches (and two divided parts of the population) was in fact insoluble.

Constantine first of all treated only the 'catholics' (Caecilians) as a church (which had financial and other consequences for them). Then when the Donatists protested, he set up an arbitration process and appointed three bishops from Gaul under the presidency of Bishop Miltiades of Rome with power to decide. When this measure failed (the Donatists, who lost, did not accept the verdict), Constantine made the same attempt with a larger court composed of representatives of all the Western churches at a synod in Arles in 314. His expectation of being able to restore unity in accordance with the Christian ethos was again disappointed. The Donatists protested, and agitated against a verdict which again went against them. The emperor now saw the matter as his immediate responsibility, convinced himself of the illegitimacy of the Donatists' position, and instituted violent action against them. Ordinances were issued against Donatist possession of churches, and because of the active resistance there was probably bloodshed. From now on the Donatists proclaimed themselves with even more force as the true, loyal martyr church which was preserving the ideal of holiness from the period of the martyrs and was again being persecuted by the new emperor.

Two things above all are significant here. 1. When the Donatists were put under pressure from the law and the police, and state intervention in the church dispute was to their disadvantage, they were the first to raise a protest which has been handed down word for word: 'What has the emperor to do with the church?' But they themselves had been the first to appeal to the emperor. This pattern was often repeated in early church history, namely that those favoured by the imperial policy found state intervention in order and were pleased at it, while those at a disadvantage not only made objections but in principle disputed the legitimacy of such intervention. We can see how the lack of a basic clarification of the question could be exploited for partisan options. 2. Just as significant is the position of the emperor and the assent of the catholic bishops to it. Constantine saw as his duty a concern for public order, which had been considerably disturbed by Donatism, at least in North Africa. And he saw order and unity being lost particularly in the sphere of the cult, which was most important for him. The church, which as the imperial religion was to share in guaranteeing the success of the Constantinian era, was putting peace at risk. The remedy lay in the competence of the emperor as the Roman state constitution knew it. And Christians, like all their contemporaries, saw Constantine's measures of religious (and now church) policy as the fulfilment of imperial duties and functions which Roman law imposed on him. But as a rule the church's assent only lasted as long as it derived an advantage and favour from him. The relationship between church and emperor was not clarified. After some years of an unsuccessful repressive policy, Constantine finally practised tolerance towards the Donatists, leaving them to God's judgment. Evidently he did not regard the use of force as an adequate permanent political instrument. Donatism lived on between toleration and persecution until the fifth century, when along with the catholic church it was exterminated by the Vandal attacks in Africa.

Constantine's measures in the so-called Arian dispute were also symptomatic of his church policy; this represented a further disillusionment of the emperor with the new religion which he had chosen as a foundation for the unity of the empire. The dispute was a dogmatic controversy over the Christian image of God or the understanding of the Trinity or the relationship between God and Jesus Christ (the Logos). The dispute had broken out in 318 in Alexandria between Bishop Alexander and the priest Arius; with much polemic, aggression and condemnation it had spread all over the empire and caused a depressing division among Christians. The Synod at Nicaea in 325, later counted as the first ecumenical council, made a decision, but was unable to end the dispute, which lasted until the end of the fourth century and then revived even after that.

When in 324 Constantine became sole ruler, Alexandria and the other regions in which this debate was being carried on came under his jurisdiction for the first time. The emperor had little understanding of the dispute, regarded the issue with which it was concerned as insignificant, constantly played down the need for discussion and urgently appealed for a will to unite immediately in a common Christian conviction. This time it was the sphere of dogma in which unity was strikingly lost. And how Constantine felt is significant for his understanding of religion and Christianity: the dispute over the relationship of the Logos to God could and indeed must immediately be ended because the confusion and division it was causing among the people were devastating. The preservation of unity was far more important to Constantine than the dogmatic clarification of the definition. Here he remained completely neutral, but underestimated the depth of the differences. For the Christian theologians in dispute the important thing was to restore the unity of the church by defining the orthodox creed, measuring all doctrines by it and excluding heretics. But it was not opportune for the emperor to exclude whole groups, because that meant a division of the population of the empire and not a policy of unification. After the failure of diplomatic attempts at mediation, Constantine then chose to tackle the matter through synods of bishops. In intention the

Council of Nicaea was the first imperial council, although the particular churches were represented in very different strengths: evidently only five participants came from the Western churches. For Constantine a settlement of the conflict was so urgent and the issue now so important that he summoned the synod near to his residence so that he could be present.

Thus the synod was wholly under his influence. Because of the emperor's firm concern to achieve unity and peace rather than the victory of one party over the other (a defeated party would mean the continuation of the conflict), there was a process of negotiation aimed at producing one formula to which the great majority of the council would assent – if in part only provisionally. Constantine convened the council, determined the ceremonial and the agenda, intervened in the debate and evidently also proposed the key term *homoousios* (the Son is of one/the same substance with/as the Father); at any rate he favoured it and carried it through, and he finally endorsed the Nicene creed.

As subsequent history shows, the council was unable to achieve the goal of peace and unity. The unity lasted for only a short time. Constantine arranged the outcome of the synod to be in keeping with a vision, an anticipation of the future: after it had ended he invited the bishops to a banquet to mark the anniversary of his accession. They reclined at table harmoniously with the emperor and listened to his words; all the discord ceased. The bishops as God's servants were helping the emperor to establish the kingdom of peace in which there were only adherents of the new religion. Emperor and church were together subjects of political action. But this remained a vision. Nicaea did not represent the end of the battle within the church to establish formulae of faith (and claims to power).

The new situation of the church can clearly be seen from the two events (the Donatist and Arian disputes): its internal problems of discipline, dogma and unity were now matters of public policy, and it was no longer left alone in solving them; indeed, soon it was not even autonomous. State and society were also interested and indeed active, in the person of the emperor. Events of church life had taken on a new frame of reference and came under influences which had hitherto been unknown. The readiness of the bishops to accept these new conditions is probably to be explained from the traditional legal and religious ideas of the society of which they too were a part; it will also have been a result of their experience of the great revolution in history which they noted first of all merely in relation to its liberating and advantageous effects for Christianity. The dilemmas only arose later. The relatively naive enthusiasm of the beginnings were also connected with an evident lack of political ethics in the church, as a result of its previous existence in a social ghetto. It had no categories and almost no patterns of reflection outside the conventional (Roman) ones into which to fit the new factors – its involvement in politics, its social role and its unity of action with state and emperor. Conversely, the emperors had their practice in politics and religion already defined in Roman tradition; in the course of time Christianity at most compelled them to make a few 'corrections'.

Church and emperor also kept continually coming into conflict in the period after Constantine; given the circumstances, such conflicts could not fail to materialize. When for example Constantine's son Constantius II (337–361) as emperor of the Eastern empire took the side of the more widely disseminated 'Arian' theology, i.e. opposition to the Council of Nicaea in the dispute over belief in the Trinity (as Constantine also did in the last years of his life), he was criticized by those who supported the council for his partisan position and his political favours. And indeed it was bishops of the Western church, who, having been summoned along with Eastern bishops for a Synod of Union (which then failed) in Serdica (Sofia) in 342 or 343, in the confusion after Nicaea, requested the emperor in writing to instruct the relevant officials to stop intervening in church life and keep to their political tasks, as though the two could be separated at that time. The dispute was one for or against Athanasius, for or against the theology of the Council of Nicaea.

This is one of the cases where apparently a separation of church and state was desired, but in fact the side not favoured by the state, though it regarded itself as orthodox, wanted to prevent the other side from being given state support so that it could itself win the day. The state, then, was expected to abstain from giving partisan support, at least in the form of tolerance for both sides. The situations became increasingly insoluble because the Christian groups could not achieve reconciliation among themselves, and each side denounced the other as heresy. Therefore the emperor, who was seeking unity, had no alternative but to offer partisan support, often by backing the majority at a time when it promised success. That is how Constantius II acted when he was made sole ruler in 350, seeing here the possibility of unifying the creed of the imperial church. A resolute 'Arian', he made the Arian creed the official one and used force to compel the bishops in the West who supported Nicaea and Athanasius to subscribe to it at the synods of Arles in 353 and Milan in 355. The emperor intervened crudely, putting pressure on bishops who opposed him and banishing them, and appointing bishops who were loyal to him. Here Constantius was merely putting into practice the traditional idea of the emperor, but now there was massive criticism and opposition within the church.

However, what people deduced from their bad experiences with a Christian emperor of another confession was not, say, the separation of state and church but the need for more precise definition of competences. They saw the emperor brutally overstepping his limits, but these limits had not been laid down; rather, they were conjured up in each instance by the party which was at a disadvantage. Those offering resistance under Constantius II who were severely punished for their resistance include, for example, bishops Ossius (Hosius) of Cordoba, Lucifer of Cagliari, Eusebius of Vercelli, Hilary of Poitiers and Paulinus of Trier.

All in all, relations between church and state did not develop in the West as they did in the East, and this continued to be the case throughout late antiquity. In brief, the bishops of the eastern part of the empire were as a rule more favourably disposed towards the policy of a state church and more ready to assent to an authoritarian understanding of the emperor. However, here too there was resistance (as in the case of Basil and Athanasius). But the Western church achieved a position which in principle was more detached and more sovereign. A series of events towards the end of the fourth century led to a demarcation or establishment of mutual claims.

Bishop Ambrose of Milan (374–397), an outstanding figure both politically and theologically, resolutely explained to the emperors of his time the church's perspective on the relationship between church and state and shaped it in practical terms. He saw that there were various possibilities in principle of delineating a sphere of autonomy for the church within which imperial competence ceased and conversely the emperor was subject to the competence of the church. This was primarily the sphere of dogma. The emperor Gratian's (367–383) rejection of the pleas of the pagan opposition to restore the altar of Victory in the senate hall (see above III, 2, c) and his rescindment of a (provisional) edict of tolerance for all the different Christian tendencies was the result of massive influence from Ambrose. Ambrose caused the emperor, who in any case was already operating in state-church style almost uncompromisingly in favour of the Nicene Creed, to act even more strictly. Here the bishop gave the emperor the task of enforcing the truth of the church's dogma by political means (including compulsion). To this end he also gave the emperor the necessary instruction on the content of orthodoxy and in all measures proceeded with the harshness of one who is certain that his own position is the only possible one. The problematical basis for this certainty was the absolute concept of a truth which did not allow anything beside itself the right to exist, since the other was error that had to be suppressed.

Another episode belongs in the same context. The emperor Valentinian II (375/383–392) required the catholics to find room in churches for Arian Christians in cities everywhere, including Milan. In what came to be called the dispute over the basilicas, Ambrose again rejected the emperor's proposal (which this time was heretical) in an absolutely uncompromising way; moreover, in the course of this controversy he formulated the theoretical reflections behind his practical positions, which were aimed at a fundamental clarification of a kind that did not yet exist. He claimed that in matters of faith bishops had to decide – not emperors, who were laymen and in some circumstances only catechumens (Ep.21). When imperial soldiers besieged his basilica in 386 he delivered a passionate address to them making the point that 'the emperor is *in* the church, not *over* the church'. Here were new notes in the controversy. Ambrose identified differences between bishop and emperor at the cost of the traditional imperial ideology.

Moreover he considerably extended the sphere of 'matters of faith', in which the church even dictated to the emperor. When in 388 Theodosius I (379–395) ordered that the bishop of Kallinikon (on the Euphrates) should finance a Jewish synagogue which had been set on fire by Christians, Ambrose thought this wrong and beyond the emperor's competence. If there was a conflict between Christianity and Judaism the (religious) alternative was a matter of truth and error, and only truth counted. Here the church had competence and the truth was normative. And in fact Ambrose forced the emperor in Milan to rescind the order. The sole competence of the emperor – also in matters of religion – based on pagan theories of rule found its limit here, but through strange, momentous maxims from the Christian bishop. He argued: 'Your motive, emperor, is a concern for public order. But which is more important, the ideal of public order or the cause of religion? The state's duty of supervision has to be subordinate to the claims of worshipping God' (Epistles 40.11). Not only tolerance, but also social peace and justice were left far behind in favour of an abstract, doctrinaire notion of the truth. Dogmatic truth as formulated by the church has absolute value in all things. It is for the church to prescribe its identity and its rights. The emperor's policy may not be governed by rival perspectives, otherwise he fails culpably in his task.

Finally, an incident of another kind also belongs here. An imperial official had been killed in the city of Thessalonika as a result of local quarrels. Theodosius inflicted a draconian punishment on the population by military force which evidently caused countless deaths. Thereupon the 'unbelievable' happened: the bishop asked the emperor to acknowledge his guilt and do church penance in public. That meant that the emperor was a layman in the church and was subject to church discipline like any other Christian. Tradition reports that in fact Theodosius submitted to the penance of the church. Dogma, discipline and sacrament do not differentiate between emperors and ordinary believers.

Ambrose wanted to differentiate clearly the spheres of competence of state and church. And it was this that gave the Western part of the imperial church its profile. It had its spheres of autonomy from the emperor, just as the state had its; however, if there were church directives, the state had to put its means and help at the disposal of the church to carry through any necessary measures. In contrast to the Eastern Byzantine pattern of total linkage between church and emperor, the aim here was relative detachment with relative equality. In this way the traditional sacral ideal of the ruler was considerably

reduced. There were spheres where the emperor had no competence. In Ambrose we also find the beginnings of a terminology for a
specific division of powers. He distinguished between the *imperium*
(of the emperor) and the *sacerdotium* (of the bishops) in order to mark
a strict division between their spheres of authority, which he saw as
being at the same time closely dependent on each other.

Ambrose did not clarify all this in controversy with a weak
emperor. Theodosius always brought the state authority of his
regime strongly to bear, even against the church and its clergy; but
evidently as one who had been baptized he accepted 'instruction'
from Bishop Ambrose. And at the same time it was through this
emperor that Christianity was definitively established in its function
as state church throughout the empire.

Augustine (354–430) must also be mentioned in connection with
the topic of church and state, not because he influenced this
relationship in any special way in his time, but because the
fundamental mediaeval ideas of order were derived from his
writings. Augustine put the state in the sphere of the provisional or
the transitory. He saw its quality as being neutral and pragmatic
and in some circumstances even sinful – depending on the
tendency of state interests (for example pride, enjoyment of power,
and vices were obviously sinful). The state was subject to the
demands of Christian morality, but according to Augustine it was
not (as others thought) directly called on to disseminate and
implement the truth (of Christianity). Its task was to order and
safeguard the conditions of life in this world. Any public help given
to the church (for example in the Donatist dispute) was not really
the duty of the state, but that of Christians in influential positions.
Where Augustine justified compulsion to faith (specifically in
protecting the general public from harm as a result of unbelief and
heresy, but above all with the success of compulsory conversion),
he was not seeking to clarify the relationship between church and
state, which does not seem to have been a direct, central problem
for him, because the state was not so important for him. Augustine
had almost 'secularized', enlightened notions of rule compared
with his pagan and Christian contemporaries: he saw the state as a
temporal, earthly thing.

However, a particular model of Augustine's thought had an

influence in quite a different direction. He interpreted the world and history in terms of the idea of two 'cities', 'states' or 'realms' (*civitates*), the 'city of God' (*civitas Dei*) and the earthly city (*terrena civitas*, also *civitas diaboli*). Although according to Augustine these do not correspond with church and state, and it will not be possible to distinguish these spheres before the end of the world (the boundaries run through all visible institutions like church and state), his idea was later understood to mean that the bisection of reality into that belonging to God and that belonging to Satan can already be identified within history and that the relationship between the state ('world') and the church can be described by the distinction between these two spheres of rule or authority. Pope Gelasius (492–496) formulated in a way which was to be normative for the subsequent period the theory of the two powers (*utraque potestas*) of the priesthood (*sacerdotium*) and the ruler (*imperium*) (*Epistle* 12). He saw 'the holy authority of the bishops' and the 'power of kings' as standing side by side with equal rights, each equipped with its own competence on the orders of Christ. Emperors and bishops recognize and need one another in their respective spheres. Earlier, Pope Leo (449–461) had already enforced this division in the political sphere. It is evident that after Leo the significance of the Roman papacy, which increased in the fifth century, reinforced the tendency of the church towards independence from the emperor (who resided in the East). Whereas in the early Byzantine empire of the East the church remained subordinate to the emperor as the supreme head of the Christian imperium, the Western church continued to emancipate itself from the emperor in Byzantium and took on a new relationship to the Germanic state, which after the migrations had established itself in the territory of the former Roman empire in the West. Pope Gregory the Great (590–604) markedly influenced this development when for primarily pastoral reasons he established relations with the Franks and West Goths. As a result the Western church was withdrawn from the protection and influence of the East Roman emperor. The encounter with the new states of the West and their Germanic notions of politics and religion gave rise to new conditions for the relationship between state and church, which helped to shape the early Middle Ages in the West.

(e) The changed church

The new conditions after Constantine left their traces on the appearance of the church. Certainly not everything that distinguishes the churches of the fourth century from those of the second or third centuries goes back to the shift under Constantine. But developments which had already begun earlier were favoured by the new circumstances. Other things were really new and different. First of all, as a body recognized under public law, a status that it had acquired by having been placed on an equal footing with the other religions in the empire, Christianity was in a position completely different from that in an earlier period, when it was a religious minority, politically suspect, socially rejected and finally persecuted by the state. Now it had a public reputation. That was visible to anyone: now its cultic buildings (basilicas) were to be found all over the cities, financed by the emperor. From 321 Sunday was a weekly Christian festival for all society, a day of rest with worship. Financial contributions from the state made numerous noticeable activities possible, especially in the social and charitable sphere. The bishops as the representatives of the new imperial religion were given the status of officials with the privileges which went with that status, like the rights of dignitaries, exemption from tax and so on. For example, in 318 they were given the right to sit in judgment in civil trials in which Christians were involved, and other legal authority. Thus at the same time they had their due place in court protocol, which again brought them titles, honours and the like. All this became visible in the insignia that they wore, like the pallium, a special headgear, their own kind of shoes, ring and so on. Depending on their rank they had the right to a throne, incense, kissing of the hand, a choir. In this way such ritual elements, still to be seen in the church today, were transferred from the court ceremonial of the emperors of late antiquity into the liturgy of the church. With these attributes of dignity they necessarily changed the understanding of the church's ministry (see Chapter IV, 2). Bishops were only recognizable as dignitaries, and no longer as servants.

But the changes went deeper. The previous section discussed the Christian adoption of what was originally the pagan sacralization of the emperor. Because the starting point was that the emperor represented God or Christ, the idea of the emperor influenced the image of God, and above all the image of Christ. So it was only natural for Christ now to be imagined and presented along imperial lines, an approach the influence of which lasted down to the high Middle Ages. Now Christ was depicted correspondingly in early Christian art as ruler, pantocrator, with the attributes of throne, raised hand, halo, palace, servants and so on. Church buildings also corresponded to this pattern: the basilica as the imperial throne room with its triumphal arch, the throne with a baldachino, the image of the pantocrator. Pictorial art of course shaped piety and the believer's relationship to Christ depicted in this way, who was worshipped with predicates of imperial dignity.

In line with the Roman understanding of religion, the Christianity of the imperial church saw itself very much as cult; and here in turn the understanding of cult was stamped more by Rome than by the New Testament and earliest Christianity. It is significant here that from the fourth century onwards the biblical justifications for cultic institutions in the church were drawn exclusively from the Old Testament, with no notice of the criticism or correction offered by Jesus or earliest Christianity. That is especially true of the notions of purity in sacrifice, priesthood and cult, which could only have been derived from the Old Testament and from outside Christianity (from Rome) because they were alien to earliest Christianity.

In church piety there was a mass of religious practices which were clearly or partly of pagan origin; they could only be introduced or preserved in so natural a way because people were living in a new era in which paganism was thought to be a thing of the past and anxiety about outside influence had largely been set aside. Relics of paganism lived on in the cult of martyrs, the dead and relics, as in pilgrimages, belief in miracles, magical customs and so on. Many bishops criticized this and called their people to real repentance, to the Christian form of the pious life. Much proved to be the result of an incomplete conversion and a defective knowledge of Christianity.

In the fourth century, the century of Constantine, the church was not just the winner; it encountered numerous problems in connection with its pastoral work, as it did over its own identity in relation to the state and society. Both bishops and communities

suffered severely under a state Christianity which was inadequate at
the level of faith and morality, and reacted to this in a variety of ways.

All in all, the changes to the church indicated here took place
slowly. But the pace accelerated under Constantine, and many new
possibilities were opened up. Taken together, they show how the
church was dovetailed into the values of its time and how it was
influenced by the political and cultural conditions of an age.

Bibliography

T. D. Barnes, *Constantine and Eusebius*, Harvard University Press 1981
N. H. Baynes, *Constantine the Great and the Christian Church*, Oxford
    University Press ²1972
C. J. Cadoux, *The Early Church and the World*, Scribner 1925
F. Homes Dudden, *The Life and Times of St Ambrose*, Oxford University
    Press 1935
Robin Lane Fox, *Pagans and Christians*, Viking 1986
W. H. C. Frend, *Martyrdom and Persecution in the Early Church*,
    Blackwell 1965
R. M. Grant, *Augustus to Constantine*, Harper and Row 1970
S. L. Greenslade, *Church and State from Constantine to Theodosius*, SCM
    Press 1956
Alistair Kee, *Constantine versus Christ*, SCM Press 1982
F. G. B. Millar, *The Emperor in the Roman World*, Duckworth 1977
N. Q. King, *The Emperor Theodosius and the Establishment of Christianity*,
    SCM Press 1961
Robert L. Wilken, *The Christians as the Romans Saw Them*, Yale
    University Press 1984

IV

Church Life and Organization

The main interest of the early Christian church lay in realizing its life as a community of believers. That came about through the building up of the communities, through organizing their life in the liturgical celebration of the mysteries of faith, through the formulation and actualization of the Christian confession, and through the ethical practice of Christianity. All this was more important for the church than establishing the principles of its relationship to society and the state and even than the systematic geographical extension of Christianity. In developing its forms of life and its confession the early church showed considerable assurance and creativity; here it was orientated on the Bible, on traditions which were growing and had grown, and on the needs of the moment.

1. The particular and local churches and their practice of unity

Wherever Christianity gained a footing, communities formed, i.e. small groups of people sharing the same conviction, the same ethos, and with an intensive group life. So the term 'church' was first of all the designation for the individual community in a particular place. That had already been the case in earliest Christianity, and it also remained the terminology of the next centuries. As the local church, the community was always the concrete entity of Christianity. It had its existence in the belief of its members in Christ, in shared baptism, in the fellowship of the eucharist, in the gifts and services of individuals, and finally in its ministries. Individual local churches did not need anything outside themselves to be churches in the full sense. But at the same time 'church' *a priori* meant the fellowship of the local churches. In a particular region they formed a church which transcended the individual community. So 'church' was also the term for all the communities in a region and indeed throughout the world. The Western, Roman tradition of church history is familiar with the picture of the whole church as a centralized organization; in other words, its legally organized and theologically centralistic authority is centred on the bishop of the community of Rome as the pope. However, this picture of the church developed only in the Western church, and here too it was not already present at the beginning, nor could it ever be established for the whole of Christianity. The church of the first centuries was like a worldwide network of local churches, differing in density from region to region, each with its bishops, and all with the same status. Focal points subsequently formed in this network and some churches became superior to others (see below, IV, 2, b and c).

Because of the independence of the individual local and particular churches, differences arose from church to church, for example in the liturgy, in which the churches had different orders, texts, dates and festivals (see below IV, 3). Similarly, the church constitution had its local peculiarities (see below IV, 2). Church discipline (how it dealt with sin and failures) was not the same everywhere. The limits of the canon of the New Testament for a long time differed from place to place. Not even the confessional formulae were identical, either in content or in formulation. And the same was true of many pious customs of the communities like prayer, fasting, penitence, etc. The theology of the early church was also equally varied. We know very different views, 'systems', traditions, perspectives and approaches from the writings of the church fathers (see Chapters VI and VII). The particular churches developed their confessions each under the conditions of its time and culture, and these were not the same, say, in Syria, Africa and Gaul.

The churches were aware of this plurality; it must have been striking in any gathering of the communities. But it was not seen as a defect in itself and it could even be said that concrete differences in church life proved the unity of Christians in faith. Understandably, however, the differences often enough gave rise to disunion, conflict and dispute. But co-ordination in all things was not a basic feature of the early church. There was a certainty that the same faith, the one proclamation of Christ, was being expressed in the different tongues of the local churches. That can be explained from the fact that all the particular churches felt that they had the same basic apostolic origin and respected one another. The most varied regional churches claimed apostolic authority for themselves, because in their city, or their land, an apostle had preached, founded the church, appointed the first bishop, died and been buried there. Thus the particular churches developed independently and individually from the conviction that they stood in the tradition of 'their' apostle: he was in accord with all the other apostles, so the churches everywhere were also in accord.

Thus unity was seen essentially in terms of an agreement in faith and the fellowship of the local and particular churches. There was a significant term for this: Latin *communio*, Greek *koinonia*. Both terms mean community, fellowship, and here denote the universality of the church in so far as all Christians everywhere belong to it in the one faith.

> In accordance with the earliest Christian meaning of the word this term *communio* meant the communion of Christians with Christ; however, this made the word a suitable term for denoting the church fellowship of Christians and the particular structure of the church.

With striking emphasis the early church saw to it that unity with Christ, the unity of Christians and the *communio* of the many individual churches, was something that could be experienced. That happened through the practice of *communio* in concrete forms. Above all the celebration of the eucharist (see below, IV, 3, b) was the way in which *communio* was achieved: unity with Christ and the unity of the church. But the context of the eucharist was the local church. *Communio* was literally achieved by Christians coming together to celebrate in the one bread and in the combination of confession and hope. So in the fourth century this word *communio/koinonia* was also used as a direct designation for the eucharist. In the large cities, in which it was no longer possible for everyone to gather in the same room because of the numbers, from the fourth century on, at least on some days in the year, there were services in which all the Christians of a city could take part (so-called station services) in order to experience their unity. We have evidence of this, for example, for

Rome, Jerusalem, Antioch and Tours. And where it was no longer possible to hold such station services because there was no church which would hold all the Christians of a city, they divided themselves among the so-called titular churches of the city, in which the eucharist was celebrated everywhere at the same time as the episcopal celebration. And as a sign of *communio* the bishop sent portions of the eucharistic bread from his celebration to the communities in the titular churches, where they were put in the eucharistic chalice as a striking demonstration of unity. We should also see in this context the custom of taking eucharist to the homes of those who were absent with good reason (a practice first attested in Justin, *Apology* I, 67, 6), and also the strict rule that sin annuls communion and thus excludes from the eucharist.

This striving for unity went beyond the local churches. Unity with other communities was also practised. One quite significant phenomenon is the extensive correspondence carried on between the churches from the first century on. The so-called First Letter of Clement, sent from Rome to Corinth around 96 CE, is the oldest example of this outside the Bible. Such letters reflect the interest of the local churches in one another. They seek to be vehicles of communication and an exchange of views, so that churches provide mutual support in a conflict or an emergency. The style of such letters differs: admonition, encouragement, criticism, correction or direction. Here there was no legal dependence of one church on another, but churches of equal rank corresponded with one another within the communion. Around 160–170 CE, Bishop Dionysius of Corinth wrote a whole series of letters to other churches, some of them far distant (in Lacedaimonia, Athens, Nicomedia, on Crete, in Asia Minor and in Rome) though he had no official responsibility for any of them. The main topics of these letters are the greatest concerns of the time: the true faith, heresy, a readiness for peace and unity and a committed Christian life of unexceptionable morality. A church being admonished was often reminded of its excellent (apostolic) origin or its former exemplary character; mutual encouragement was given in tricky situations by praise and consolation; instructions were conveyed in the interpretation of the Bible or holy asceticism; there were pastoral guidelines, and so on. Moreover information was exchanged about the death or election of a bishop, about persecutions which had been withstood, about threats from new heresy, and the like; questions were asked and advice was given.

Such correspondence could create solidarity and familiarity, lead to mutual acquaintance and establish closer relations. Significantly the churches regarded the letters as documents with an importance going beyond their immediate occasion, and they were regularly read out in the assembly as a living act of communion. And because the letters could not be sent by official post, they provided even closer contacts between the communities. They were delivered by Christians who were travelling on business or had been sent specifically. These messengers came to the communities and were given lodging there free of charge, so that there was communication and communion. Hospitality was one of the common virtues of the early church which was valued highly; as a Christian practice it was at the same time a further form of communion in faith. In order to exclude misuse, a bishop would give a Christian of his community going on a journey a letter to be his credentials for communities abroad. This was called a *communio* letter, a letter of commendation or peace. Such a document not only had practical advantages but also guaranteed the regular creation of numerous contacts between communities and individual Christians.

However, there was a problem with this practice, namely that in the course of time bishops had set themselves outside the communion by heresy or sin, so that their letters of commendation were no longer accepted. Consequently lists of orthodox bishops now had to be made in the communities, so that the communion would not be undermined. This experience that communion could be broken by sin or dispute was a great burden for the churches. Communion as unity and peace was at the same time both a reality and a task. As is well known, the whole church could not maintain its communion, but in the course of history split into different churches (see Chapter V).

Communion was broken not only between local and particular churches but also within the individual community as a result of sin and heresy. The church practised excommunication, exclusion from communion. In the church structure described above, anyone who was in communion could break it off for an appropriate reason: bishops from laity, presbyters or another bishop; and in some circumstances the laity or the community from their bishop, though of course this was the exception. The possibility of mutual excommunication led to unmistakable confusions and unedifying developments. Communion and excommunication were abused as tactical weapons in disputes over power and doctrine. Coupled with this was the problematical principle of making the limits of church communion also the limits of Christian understanding and reconciliation.

This practice of the unity of local and particular churches also included the holding of synods or councils (see Chapter VIII, 1). Countless synods were held from after the second half of the second century. They were gatherings at which neighbouring churches from a smaller or larger area or later – at any rate in principle – from all the churches of the inhabited world were represented above all by their bishops to discuss questions of church order, doctrine, liturgy and discipline which had become acute. These common decisions led to a common practice in which the unity of the local churches was manifested. They were communicated by letter to all churches elsewhere. The historical occasion for the first synods, in the latter part of the second century, was evidently the rise of Montanism as a separate Christian movement, i.e. a heresy, and also a dispute between the particular churches over the date of Easter, a problem of the uniformity of church ritual. Even if they could not always resolve all differences finally, the synods were the ideal instrument for realizing or rescuing communion in difficult situations. The assembled episcopate represented the church united (or divided) beyond one particular place. Where a dispute remained unresolved, the majority required the minority to submit to its view (in some cases unsuccesfully) in order to preserve communion. However, the practice of holding synods resulted in bishops and local churches acquiring different degrees of authority because the bishops of large cities necessarily tended to become leaders of the churches in their region (see IV, 2, b below).

2. *The development of church order*

Our earliest sources, the New Testament writings, report relatively little about church order and organization in the earliest Christian period; other topics were more important to them. Moreover, the church discovered its forms of organization and order in the sacramental and legal sense of later periods only in the course of history, and also varied them. In the earliest period we should suppose such elements to have developed only to a very limited degree. For developments in the first decades by no means took place in the expectation of a long future for the church, so there was no interest in a lasting order. However, earliest Christianity already knows a series of elements of order, even if they were of a different quality from the institutions which were to develop from them in the course of history.

(a) Ministries in the church

In the earliest Christian communities there were necessarily different levels of responsibility. These were orientated on the way in which the community understood itself, its functions and the tasks which arose. The biblical writings indicate various early groups of authorities. The oldest group of prominent men in the earliest church was the Twelve (apostles). In all historical probability they go back to Jesus (Mark 3.14), but according to the Gospels they had the symbolic function of being representatives of the old and the new Israel (cf. Matt. 19.28). There is no evidence anywhere of the Twelve holding office in the church, and strikingly there is no historical information about the majority of them for the period after Jesus' death (there are only later legends).

Things are different with the group of authorities formed by James, Peter and John. According to Paul (Gal. 2.9) they were regarded as the 'pillars' in Jerusalem; in other words, they were the key figures in the community there. They were evidently the authoritative spokesmen (Gal. 2.12). James was a brother of Jesus, and Peter and John came from the group of Twelve. Finally there was the group of the 'Seven' in Jerusalem, men with exclusively Greek names whom Acts (6.1–6) made into the seven deacons, though in reality they may have been the leading body of the 'Hellenists' among the first followers of Jesus in Jerusalem (see Chapter I, 3), and thus a group of authorities.

The authority of these people in the earliest church was based in the case of the Twelve on the fact that they had lived with Jesus, had been commissioned by him and moreover were witnesses of his resurrection (I Cor.15.5). That also applies to two of the three 'pillars', Peter and John; Paul (I Cor.15.7) knows that James, who had not been one of the Twelve, was also witness to the resurrection, and his kinship with Jesus was certainly also a factor in his role. Finally, the Seven were the leaders and spokesmen of the Hellenistic Christians in Jerusalem – we do not know how they acquired this status. And a little later Paul quite specifically derives his own authority as an apostle from a direct commission from the risen Christ.

So the derivations of authority differ, and the kinds of competence and responsibility we have here are strictly speaking unrepeatable; they cannot be described as ministry in the legal and sacramental sense. In the case of the apostles and the witnesses to the resurrection we have a singular authority deriving from the origins of the faith, and with the Seven a pragmatic solution to the task of leadership in a bilingual community. Of course the testimony of the Jerusalem authorities to the resurrection was of abiding significance for all communities and could never be surpassed, but it was impossible to hand down this quality of being a witness; in earliest Christianity it never resulted in a permanent 'office' or the like, or say in a legal, institutional predominance of Jerusalem over the churches now coming into being; it was always 'only' a 'bond of love' (e.g. in the form of a collection for the Jerusalem church, Rom.15.25–27; I Cor.16.1–3; II Cor.8.19; Gal.2.10; Acts 24.17) and thus not a special institutional relationship.

The authorities listed above were not the only ones in the course of the expansion of Christianity. The communities needed local authorities, responsible leaders for their communal life. Developments in this area did not take the same form everywhere, because they did not run either in accordance with a given programme or under central direction, but were regulated in accordance with the demands and possibilities of the time. The forms of leadership and designations of the authorities differed. However, it seems always to have been the case that in the early period the individual community was not governed by an individual leader but by a 'college', a group of responsible persons. The Acts of the Apostles (11.30; 15; 21.18, etc.) shows that in the Palestinian communities these people were called presbyters (elders). The form and designation was an obvious one; Judaism had this form of collegial leadership and in it the 'elders' as a group had a leading position. Christians, former Jews, as a matter of course took over this order, which they knew. So the presbyters had the task of organizers.

Things were different for Paul and his mission territories. Paul saw himself both as their original apostolic authority and also as having the role of one who was the direct authority in an individual community on questions of preaching and discipline. But he could not be everywhere at the same time. There were responsible representatives in his communities. Two things are then striking: Paul does not call these representatives presbyters, but has a variety of terms for them, some interchangeable, some indicating differences. For example, he calls the same people 'labourers', 'fellow workers' (I Cor.16.16), 'leaders' (I Thess.5.12; Rom.12.8), but on the other hand distinguishes between apostles, prophets and teachers (I Cor.12.28), who have different tasks. We do not find a single concept of ministry in Paul, but designations of tasks, positions and functions in the community. The position of those responsible for particular tasks was not based on law and institutional authority, but was understood as service (*diakonia*), by Paul as later in the Gospels (Rom.12.7; I Cor.3.5; 12.5; II Cor.1.24; 5.18; Mark 10.42–45; Matt.23.1–12).

> Certainly the Pauline church did not represent an enthusiastic chaos of charismatics; there were leaders and there was order in it. However, Paul did not react to conflicts by building up authority and ministry, but by describing the multiplicity of gifts and requiring that all should use their spiritual gifts for the edification of the church (and not in rivalry, I Cor.12; 14). Certainly Paul emphasized his personal authority over a rebellious community often enough and with unprecedented sharpness (I Cor.4.21; II Cor.13.2–4, 10). But here the issue was his status as apostle and the establishment of the gospel (free of the Law), and not the constitution of the church.

At one point in his extant letters Paul terms the leaders and their helpers 'bishops and deacons' (Phil.1.1). These must be 'overseers' (the significance of the term bishop) and organizers, which does not yet have much to do with the power of the later bishop (see below). In Paul they supervised the communities and their lives.

There is an important distinction here: earliest Christianity knew two different forms or orders of community, the presbyteral form, which was of Jewish origin and occurred above all in communities in the Jewish sphere, and the episcopal form, in the Pauline communities. It is important to note that both had a collegial structure: a leading body performed the tasks of leadership. In the one case it consisted of presbyters, and in the other of bishops (*episkopoi*).

The initial conditions, with the expectation of an imminent end to the world, in which constitution and organization could be only of relative importance, came to an end. The apostles and the first generations died out. The time of earliest Christianity had passed. Around the beginning of the second century this gave rise to a new mentality, new needs and necessities. And these were clearly expressed in the development of the ministry and order of the church. An abiding church in an abiding world had to organize itself for the long term. Questions of organization became more important than before. Now the task of the leaders became the church's ministry, an established institution with a sacral character, with an authority in questions of teaching and discipline derived from the apostles. Ministers were solemnly appointed to their offices by ordination; ordination consisted in the sacramental transfer of official powers (consecration as a ritual means of conveying the Spirit). Ministers were guarantors of doctrine, part of the chain of those who handed down the gospel from the beginning (I Clement, I and II Timothy, Titus). Thinking was organized in an institutional and legal way, aimed at safeguarding the identity of Christianity, and was accelerated by the rise of deviations (heresy).

In time circumstances required a unification of church order. So at first we find mixed forms with elements of both presbyteral and episcopal order. Some sources (Acts; I and II Timothy; Titus; I Clement; letters of Ignatius; letter of Polycarp to the Philippians) know both presbyters and bishops at the same time, though it is difficult to reconstruct the relationship between the two. However, at any rate the differentiation in rank between the existing offices, i.e. the beginnings of hierarchy, are connected with this. And an important phenomenon was that now images of the church became dominant in which theologically the ministry obscured the community level.

This early Christian move towards a clear institutionalization, towards a constitution, the forming of sacral law and a sacramental concept of the ministry, was something new in early church history. Historical theology talks of the rise of early catholicism. This term is a most apt description of the new period which marked the transition from earliest Christianity to the catholic church of the following centuries.

However, 'early catholicism' is often meant as a criticism of this development; in principle it is thought to have been decadent. The charismatic community, as earliest Christianity understood it, living by the spirit of the gospel and immediately responsible to Christ, is said to have been replaced by an organized church with legal structures of authority and subordination; the free offer of the gospel is said to have become a doctrine administered by a ministry and tied to the institution, turned into dogmatic statements of a legal character presented to individuals as being that on which their salvation or damnation depended. However, these sweeping comments and this critical assessment of developments overlook the fact that earliest Christianity was not in principle incompatible with the development of a constitution, ministry, etc.; rather, it had its own elements of order. Moreover, there was not, nor is there, any alternative in principle to such institutionalization. However, its concrete forms were not fixed historically in advance. What actually happened had never been laid down in any binding way, so hypothetically other developments were also conceivable. But what developed, and in the cause of church history also changed again, cannot be described after the event as a 'divine institution' of a mythical kind and back-dated to Jesus or the apostles. Certainly it was the early church itself which claimed that what had come about had been instituted by Jesus and the apostles, but it did not do this, as we now know, on the basis of historical recollection, but under the influence of leading theological ideas according to which the apostles left behind the church in the form in which it was known later. The order of the early church with its constitution and ministries was not the beginning but the result of a development. And if one can say that in principle there was no alternative to this historical development in the direction of so-called early catholicism, this is in the sense that any religion needs tradition and institution to communicate itself. Here what is communicated is more important than the organ by which it is communicated. And in Christianity the relationship between ministry and gospel is subject to the criteria of service and the cross, excluding domination (Mark 10.42–45; II Cor.1.24), but not authority. And it is of course the case that not all the structures which came into being stand up to the early Christian maxim that the ministry and constitution of the church must have the character of *diakonia* if it is to be possible to relate them to Jesus.

Along with the late New Testament writings, I Clement (c.96–98) is a typical example of this early catholicism in the post-apostolic period. It calls the leaders overseers (1.3), bishops (42.2) or presbyters (44.5), and for the first time gives them a function in worship, namely the 'offering of the gifts' (44.4). But above all, here we find the influence of the idea mentioned above that the apostles instituted the ministries of the church directly. It is concluded from this that the concrete order of the church is eternally unassailable, unchangeable and ultimately the will of God, sacral. The reaction of the community must be one of obedience to the presbyters. Thus what had come about in history was given a theological foundation and immunized against change. From now on the quality of apostolicity (as a historical and dogmatic basis for the structure of the church) played a paramount role for both the constitution and the teaching of the church. A further example is the Didache or 'Teaching of the Twelve Apostles', a work composed around 140 CE in Syria which contains a so-called church order, i.e. regulations for church life. It provides the interesting information about the history of the church's ministry that in its time there were prophets, teachers and apostles who were not attached to a single place but were itinerant ministers, visiting the communities (11; 13.1–2). There is a request that bishops and deacons should be chosen within a locality; so here they are being introduced for the first time: this is so that they can be permanent presences and also take over the task of instruction (15.1). We come across the phenomenon of a twofold order of ministry with both itinerant ministers (prophets, teachers, apostles) and local ministers (bishops, deacons). Here we have a reflection of an early stage with election by the community (instead of appointment).

The period of early catholicism can be put between late in the first century and the middle of the second. Thus, say, in the writings of Bishop Irenaeus (Eirenaios) of Lyons, in Gaul, around 185 CE we find the institutionalization of responsibility for the teaching of the faith fully developed: to distinguish truth from heresy Irenaeus developed the principle of reserving the truth exclusively for the bishops (and teachers) of the church, because they alone took over the truth from the apostles and preserved it. In unbroken succession, each bishop was in accord with the first occupant of his throne, and the first bishop had been appointed directly to it by an apostle (or disciple of the apostles). This construction of historical continuity now guaranteed orthodoxy with the help of the ministry.

The church order of Bishop Hippolytus(?) of Rome shortly after 200 then shows what further documents confirm: ministry fanned out, again differently, depending on the particular church, into a multiplicity of tasks, functions and even states, so that the concept and delimitation of ministry is often not easy to indicate. As well as bishops, presbyters and deacons (now in this order) there were also confessors, widows, lectors, virgins, subdeacons, teachers, acolytes, exorcists and ostiaries (doorkeepers). However strict the definition of the ministry, in the second and third centures there was still a certain breadth and lines were not clearly drawn. In the early period women also had ministries (leadership, prophecy), but only in the early period. And with Hippolytus there is also a sharp sub-division of the community into clergy and laity on the basis of ordination (*Apostolic Tradition* 8–10,19). In his case there is a striking change in vocabulary; his church order speaks of the ministry less in terms of service and more in terms of lordship and rule. Between the second and the fourth century the theological understanding of church ministry became increasingly cult-related: with recourse to Old Testament ideas, bishops and presbyters were increasingly understood as priests who offer the eucharist as a sacrifice (cf. Chapter III,

2, e). The origin of the celibate ministry, the early traces of which go back to the fourth century, is to be explained from the Old Testament concept of the cultic purity of the priest, which is connected with this.

Within the changing history of constitutional order in the early church the office of bishop developed as the central and most important of all ministries. As has already been indicated, its beginnings were not striking. The office of bishop was originally an office of oversight, i.e. a number of men, a college of bishops, was entrusted with tasks of organization and adminstration in the community. In the course of history further responsibilities were then transferred to this ministry, beginning with that of teaching (Didache 15.1), so that in time the office of bishop became the most powerful and important ministry. By the third century it had developed into the form in which it has shaped church order down to the present day, namely the office of the monarchical bishop. This term denotes the single bishop who is over a community (no longer a college of several bishops).

The seven letters of Ignatius of Antioch are the earliest known evidence for the existence of the monarchical episcopate. Ignatius, himself a monarchical bishop in Antioch, similarly presupposed this office in the five churches of Asia Minor to which he wrote his letters between 115 and 117, in Ephesus, Magnesia, Tralles, Philadelphia and Smyrna. We do not know how developments reached this point. It is certain that at the same time elsewhere, for example in Rome, there were still collegial forms of church government. But the development of church ministries followed different courses at different rates. During the second century the office of monarchical bishop then became established in a uniform way in all the particular churches. It is important that (already with Ignatius) one bishop symbolizes the unity of the community, as does his presiding at the eucharist; in every respect the bishop is the centre and the head of the community, which follows him. The presbyters are under the bishop as a group on their own and so are the deacons. The way in which this hierarchy and structure of ministry is justified is important: this church is a copy or continuation on earth of the order in heaven. In different ways Ignatius derives a church order with bishops, priests and deacons from the heavenly order of God – Christ – the apostles.

In the early period, this was an extraordinarily effective pattern as a basis and authority for church order: church order corresponds to, is a copy of, the heavenly order, is willed by God in that way and not otherwise, and is therefore unassailable. An ethic for ministry and community in which some are set over others was derived from this. The theological idea of the representation of the heavenly hierarchy by the church hierarchy even had a great influence on mediaeval ideas of order through Pseudo-Dionysius (around 500 CE). Such notions are not limited to Ignatius in the early church. The bishop acts 'in God's place', the community obeys him as God (e.g. Magnesians 6.1; 7.1). The one bishop acts as the image of the one God and guarantees the unity of the church in times of threat. So there may only be one bishop who guides the local church, because otherwise the image of God and the unity of the church are not clear. Because of the monarchical episcopate, the early church was very much a closed society and capable of resistance. The unity of doctrine and cult under the one bishop made it possible to lead the individual community effectively.

The derivation of church order from heavenly order is a different kind of theological justification from basing it on apostolic succesion or appointment by the apostles. In the early church the more widespread picture is of the bishops as successors to the apostles, but the idea of the parallelism between the heavenly hierarchy and the church hierarchy is equally old. In both ways the church constitution is in retrospect endorsed theologically as the only conceivable and legitimate one, a constitution which has always been like that and is unchangeable. Thus in the second century the bishop guaranteed the purity of doctrine, led the community, watched over church discipline and thus over admission to the eucharist, presided at the eucharist and in his person symbolized unity. Moreover in the third century (in Hippolytus's church order) it is said of him that he offers God the sacrifice of the church, ordains men as clergy and forgives sins (thus has the authority to impose penance). The bishop is now primarily the leader and high priest of his church.

Bishop Cyprian of Carthage in North Africa was a particularly important theologian and organizer of the episcopate in the middle of the third century. For him the church was an episcopal church and the episcopate the principle of the church. Here, too, the bishop guaranteed unity and peace, and at the same time he safeguarded the link between the local church and the whole church. Furthermore, Cyprian grounded the unity *between* bishops in Peter: this office began with Peter (chronologically before the other apostles); therefore he has a chronological and ideal priority to them all, and as an individual figure symbolizes the unity of the episcopate. Matthew 16.18f. is to be related to any church; any bishop is Peter, and the foundation of his church (*De ecclesiae unitate* 4f.). The 'mutual harmony' of the bishops is the performance of the ministry of Peter as the unity of the whole church. The office of bishop is a ministry of unity. The reason why Cyprian stresses unity so strongly is evident from the situation: in the period of persecution under Decius there were various views about the possibility of receiving the many apostate Christians back into the church. The rigorists excluded any possibility of this, but those who were tolerant wanted to grant it without any great fuss. In this disunity Cyprian gave sole responsibility to the bishop: he alone is normative, i.e. he also has penitential power, imposes a strict procedure for penance, and decides whether the lapsed are to be readmitted. Cyprian further strengthened this office through theology and church practice.

So the office of bishop became the central office of the church through a steady accrual of tasks, competences and power. The bishop embodied virtually all church functions and authorities. This did not come about without resistance to the idea of church authority bound up with it and led to the loss of schismatic churches (Chapter V).

The structure of the church as communion (see above IV, 1) provided for all Christians to be in fellowship and share in what happened in the local community. Thus we know that between the third and the fifth centuries the congregations of great and important particular churches like Rome, Africa, Spain were involved in the election of a new bishop. The influence of the people may have been in assenting to or rejecting candidates proposed by the clergy. The purpose of this participation was to find a suitable bishop. Ordination to the ministry was not regarded as irrevocable, 'indelible', as in the sense which became customary later. The deposition of bishops for heresy or other defects in 'holiness' was by no means unusual. Finally, a change in the structure of the church as communion came about through the later history of the episcopate, namely in the mutual relationship between churches of equal status. The 'symmetry' was distorted, because soon not all bishops were of equal rank, and along with their bishops particular churches took on greater or lesser importance. Causes for difference of rank between bishops were the differing degrees of illustriousness in the past of their churches (whether or not a church had been founded by an apostle) or differences in the political status of cities (cf. IV, 1 and IV, 2, b).

The bishops of the early church represented the leading class of a church expanding in difficult circumstances. Many of them are known to us as educated men, outstanding theologians and writers, and realistic and capable (church) politicians and church leaders. Moreover, as representatives of a Christianity which was making its mark they had a reputation in non-Christian society. As prominent figures they were often the first to be affected by persecution, but we also have instances of the high social standing of bishops in the period before Constantine. And from Constantine onwards bishops had to fulfil the new expectations of society (see Chapter III, 2).

(b) The origin of the patriarchates

From the beginning of its history onwards, in its geographical expansion the church had a degree of regional division or organization. And this division *a priori* coincided almost completely with the political division of the Roman empire into provinces, which was evidently the most natural way. Just as the political and social life of the provinces was concentrated in their capitals, so too the Christian community of a capital was the centre for the Christians of a province. And just as the different cities ranked differently in the political order, so too did their churches: a hierarchy arose within them which corresponded to that in politics.

This development continued even when the church began to organize itself on a larger scale, because the scale of its communication and its problems also increased. From the third century on, the synods were convened and held in the relevant provincial capital, under the leadership of the bishop there, who thus gained a kind of pre-eminence over the provincial bishops. This corresponded precisely to political practice, according to which the jurisdiction of the authorities in the provincial capital held for the whole province. The institution of the metropolitan came into being: he was a bishop with precedence over the other bishops in his area. He supervised discipline, had high legal competence within the church, supervised and confirmed the election of bishops, and summoned and guided synods for the whole province. At the end of the developmemt (around 400), every province had its metropolitan and every metropolitan a province (just one). This organization, which had grown up pragmatically, was often endorsed by councils and popes. One possible factor in the development was that as a rule the surrounding countryside was Christianized from the cities and therefore a dependent relationship continued.

When in 325 the Council of Nicaea confirmed the order of metropolitans (canon 4), at the same time it confirmed a further order of magnitude, an already existing church structure extending beyond the metropolitans. The council stated (canon 6) that the 'old order' was to be preserved, according to which the Bishop of Alexandria and the Bishop of Rome, and also the churches of Antioch and churches of other provinces, had supreme power over several areas and not just one province. So this had already long been the case, and the sole reason for it was that it too corresponded with the facts. Here too the church structure resembled the organization of the empire. The empire was divided into dioceses, each with several provinces, each diocese govered by a senior official. This assimilation was so much the principle that as a rule the church followed state administrative reforms by changing its own administrative divisions. So in the long run the bishops of the larger cities were by no means metropolitans of equal rank. And the development just outlined resulted in the division of the early church into patriarchates, each with a patriarch at its head (these terms were customary from the sixth century onwards). In the course of time five cities achieved a status achieved by no other: Alexandria, Antioch, Rome, Constantinople and lastly Jerusalem. So in the early church there were four patriarchates in the East; Rome was the only patriarchate in the West. This position of the 'great metropolitan', later also called patriarch, also came about by the principle of adaptation to the administrative units of the empire and because of the usefulness of such hierarchical structures. In the course of time the competences of metropolitan and patriarch in the ordination and deposition of bishops, the presidency of synods, and decisions in disputes and criminal matters had to be regulated.

How did the patriarchate originate? So large an association of churches seems to have been formed first in Egypt, which was a unitary and relatively self-contained land. At least from the third century on, Alexandria was the church metropolis of all the Egyptian provinces, in other words a 'patriarchate'. Between the third and the fifth centuries the Alexandrian church was the norm for the whole of Egypt in matters of discipline and faith. Antioch did not have so coherent a background of cultural and political unity and therefore attained this central significance only later. We shall be discussing the special role of Rome separately (Chapter IV, 2, c), but here it may be noted that there was every reason for it also to attain prominent significance in the church in its character as capital of the empire and – still initially – residence of the emperor. Jerusalem had lost any special significance for Christianity as a result of the two Jewish wars (66–70 and 132–135 CE). But in the fourth century, as a result of Constantine and in the course of the pilgrimages to the Holy Land and the piety associated with them, it then attained a prominent position which it had not had in history and which had no significance in church politics either. Still, Jerusalem was a patriarchate over the three Palestinian provinces. Finally, Constantinople also became a patriarchate. Constantine, the first Christian emperor, had built this city as a Christian imperial city and in 330 had it consecrated as the 'Second (or New) Rome'. Already before Constantine, Rome had ceased to be the residence of the Roman emperor (this was Milan, Trier or Nicomedia). Here, too, the political status was decisive: the bishop of the 'New (Christian) Rome' necessarily became pre-eminent. Initially this had nothing to do with rivalry between Constantinople and the old Rome; rather, the rivalry was with Alexandria. Yet the tragic developments which led to the separation between the Eastern and the Western churches is associated with the history of this patriarchate. The rivalry between the patriarchs of the old and the new Rome is one of the historical causes of the schism, the final completion of which is dated to the year 1054.

Thus the origin of the five ancient patriarchates is to be explained in political and pragmatic terms. But here too we have the phenomenon of historical developments being subsequently given a theological derivation and basis as a safeguard. This usually took place in a situation of dispute and rivalry. Any claim had to be capable of being derived from apostolic origins. Here it seems that to begin with only the bishops of Rome stressed the theological or apostolic foundation of their pre-eminence. In the West, where Rome alone was regarded as an apostolic foundation (by Peter), the significance of apostolicity was generally put much higher in church-political terms than in the churches of the East, in which there were numerous local traditions going back to the apostles (e.g. for Corinth, Philippi, Ephesus, Gortyna). The very number of such traditions relativized apostolicity as a characteristic. But when for example Rome rejected the church-political claims made by Constantinople after the fourth and fifth centuries, appealing to its origin in the apostle Peter, the principle of apostolicity was exploited on the other side, demonstrably from the seventh and eighth centuries on, and the legend was told of the foundation of the church in Constantinople (Byzantium) by the apostle Andrew; this was believed to put Constantinople above Rome, because according to John 1.40–42 Andrew, the apostle of Constantinople, had become an apostle before Peter. Moreover Constantinople claimed the apostle John for itself. At that time historical legitimation was derived from such 'arguments'.

The history of the patriarchates was largely a history of competition and rivalry which was often accompanied by disputes over dogmatic trends with mutual excommunications and the like, or it showed itself in influence on the occupation of sees and in other measures of political power. Rome derived a claim to primacy in the universal church by virtue of its status as a patriarchate and its apostolic Petrine tradition. The churches of the East, i.e. the patriarchates, did not recognize this claim. It can be said that here there was a clash between two different and incompatible notions of church unity. Because in the East several different local churches with traditions of apostolic origin existed side by side, church unity here could never be centred on a single pre-eminent bishop; it had to consist in the unity of several patriarchates. Things were different for the church of the West. It was natural for it to safeguard the unity of the whole church under the one bishop of Rome, who was the only bishop in the West to be a patriarch and the successor of an apostle (Peter). Different constitutional forms of the church could develop from the perspectives and traditions of the particular churches and be given a theological foundation in them.

(c) The history of the primacy of Rome

From the third century on, the bishops of Rome had laid explicit claim to a pre-eminence which transcended the region and then applied to the whole church. In the course of history this led to the Roman papacy. According to the Western Latin understanding of the church, the primacy of the bishop of Rome consists in a central office of leadership for the whole church which the pope holds as successor to Peter as the 'first bishop of Rome'.

> Historically we have to reconstruct the origin and history of this pre-eminence of the pope over all bishops as reliably as possible, and see it in the context of the overall constitution and structure of the churches in the first century as these have emerged from the description so far. In the previous section it became clear that the Western church with its one apostolic foundation (Rome) tended towards a centralistic constitution under the one patriarch in Rome, whereas the Eastern church with its many apostolic traditions could not have had occasion to organize itself around a single place and a single bishop. Rome's unrivalled status in the West seems to have played a major role in the development of the theological self-understanding of the Roman bishop, as of course did also the cultural, political and ideological status of the city and its aura as 'head' of the empire.

The traditional theological justification of the Roman papacy normatively relates to the 'institution' or ordaining of this office 'by Christ' and also to the fact that Peter was the 'first bishop of Rome', and finally to the unbroken succession of bishops who are attested as the 'successors' to Peter and as such perform the functions and authorities that Peter had as the first supreme head of the whole church. The historical value of these statements needs to be discussed.

In the traditional basis for the primacy this 'institution by Christ' (what is meant is institution by the historical Jesus) is primarily guaranteed to be historical by Matt.16.18–19 and John 21.15–17. Here it must be noted as an assured result of biblical exegesis that both these biblical texts are statements of early Christian theology and not historical sayings of Jesus. And as such, along with other New Testament texts they prove only that the figure of Jesus had a pre-eminent significance in earliest Christianity.

However, this significance originally had nothing to do with the papacy. It consisted in the fact that in earliest Christianity Peter (with his symbolic name 'rock') became the representative of a church 'office' of proclamation, a symbol for all disciples and missionaries. There was no individual, special, Petrine office (papacy) as an office of leadership in the early church, nor can it yet be recognized here as an intention ('foundation'). When the Roman primacy developed later (see below), the connection between the biblical passages about Peter and the Roman papacy was made. Both the biblical texts mentioned had a meaning for the early church (in the West as well) before there was a papacy.

The statement that Peter was the first bishop of Rome arose in the second century and at that time was motivated by dogma. While we know with a considerable degree of certainty that Peter was in Rome and was a martyr, nothing is known about his activity in the city and about his role in the Roman community. That he was its bishop can be ruled out, since it is quite certain from the history of the monarchical episcopate (see above IV, 2, a) that there were not yet individual bishops in Rome or in other particular churches, but that there was always a college of bishops. The monarchical episcopate evidently developed even later in the West than in the East. (It is striking that in his letter to Rome in about 115 Ignatius of Antioch uniquely presupposes that there is no monarchical bishop of the church which he is addressing.)

Finally, as for the traditional list of all the bishops of Rome since

Peter, while there is certainly a list of their names (in Irenaeus, *Adversus haereses* III, 3, 3), it was made only in the later second century and is based on theological notions, not on historical research.

In the late second century the Western church derived its apostolicity from Peter (and Paul) in Rome. Here it presupposed for the initial conditions in the church what it knew from its own time (a monarchical bishop) and safeguarded its own tradition of faith through a list of names of bishops since Peter, though this list was first constructed on the basis of this need. Recourse to Peter was the regional (Western church) version of the proof from apostolicity. So in the second century it does not yet have anything to do with a Petrine Roman primacy over the whole church. In the East the same practice prevailed with the names of likely apostles.

The existence of a central office of leadership for the whole church was hardly compatible with the initial church structure of many apostolic foundations of equal rank and the communion of all churches. Considerable changes were needed to make possible the primacy of an individual church over many or all other churches. The shifts in the structure of the communion, through which individual churches became more or less important, had to take place. So the conditions for a church centralism did not yet exist in the early period of the church.

It is therefore not surprising that the beginnings of the Roman papacy are not to be found before the middle of the third century. Certainly, towards the end of the second century Victor I of Rome (189–199) wanted to enact a decree sweepingly relating to the whole church, in the dispute over Easter (see Chapter V), but we do not know how he formulated his claim to authority and what justification he gave for it, and this claim was criticized and rejected. It remains doubtful whether this event is part of the history of the primacy. The first certain expression of the claim of a Roman bishop to primacy was made, rather, in the middle of the third century. In the dispute over heretical baptism at this time (see Chapter V), Bishop Stephen I of Rome (254–57) attempted to impose his view by describing himself as Peter's successor to the see of Rome and as the preeminent bishop who was leader of all the churches. At the same time he was also the first to use the text Matthew 16.18f. in his argument for this Roman claim. Vigorous objections were made by various particular churches, and his view was not recognized anywhere.

Things first changed in the course of the late fourth century. Damasus I of Rome (366–384) took various initiatives to increase the significance and rank of his see. He attempted this partly through the emperor, and had considerable success. From his time on, the Roman see has been called the *Sedes Apostolica*. For example, his authority over synods (recognition by the Bishop of Rome) was extended. From now on Rome (also through Damasus) set itself above the Eastern patriarchs, with the help of the Petrine principle, which made Rome 'unique': Peter was the first among the apostles, so his successors have pre-eminence over all bishops. By contrast, from the Eastern perceptive Rome remained one patriarchate among others, to which appeal was occasionally made in conflicts, without any recognition of its general claim to primacy. Such appeals, which were made when the bishop or patriarch was unable to reach agreement, were heard by the Roman bishop as mediator. Damasus also included Matthew 16.18f. among his arguments, and really understood himself as pope. He found new ways of expressing the Roman claim, and his theological arguments took on a legal style. The forms of authoritarian decree customary in the sphere of politics were adopted: now the papal chancellery spoke in the style of imperial decretals, i.e. in the official tone of command of decrees and edicts. That was especially the case under Pope Siricius I (384–399), who developed the papacy further. The claims of these Roman bishops to primacy were only partially recognized (even in the West), but they had a long-term effect. Those who advanced them included Innocent I (402–417) and Boniface I (418–422), who chose the political category of imperial power (supreme authority, highest position) to denote the position of the bishop of Rome. The language and concepts indicated the self-understanding and practice of the holder of the office.

At the end of late antiquity, in the fifth century, there were political and historical conditions which proved extraordinarily favourable for the development of the papacy. The Western empire was occupied in the course of the migrations and divided into new kingdoms. A political vacuum arose for the indigenous Roman population: the empire had been destroyed, and there was no emperor in the West. And it was the Roman church under the leadership of Pope Leo I (440–461) who succeeded the emperor and the *imperium*. This new political role which accrued to the pope led to a major revaluation of his position and the ideology behind it. At the same time Leo I also gave decisive theological backing to this ideology, by emphasizing the Petrine character of Rome and using Matthew 16.18f. He claimed full authority (*plenitudo potestatis*) for the successors of Peter over all other bishops and over the universal church. At the Fourth Ecumenical Council of Chalcedon in 451 he was able to bring his reputation and his theology to bear in a central dogmatic decision which concerned the whole church (see Chapter VIII, 7). At the same time his idea of the papacy was also clearly marked by elements of the pagan idea of Rome, with notions and concepts drawn from the imperial Roman ideology. The pope became a powerful figure with a corresponding court ceremonial. By contrast, with Pope Gregory I (590–604) we once again find elements of a different self-understanding. He called himself the 'servant of the servants of God', thus returning to the earliest Christian notions of *diakonia* in church ministry; he also called himself 'Christ's representative'. But Gregory too used imperial insignia, attributes and titles. The popes had political power, and in both East and West (the kingdom of the Franks) came into conflict with the state authorities.

Although the Roman papacy never succeeded in imposing its claim on the whole church (in the East it was rejected in principle by most churches), at the beginning of the Middle Ages the popes had the utmost significance as spiritual, religious and political powers for the history and church history of the West. So developments in that direction continued in the fourth and fifth centuries, with their background in the church, in politics, culture and sociology, and led to a church office the holders of which were set high above the people, just as the emperor had been beforehand. This centralist and monarchical position represented by the papacy in the organizational form or constitution of the (Western) church represents a considerable change from a church organization with a synodical constitution and its structure as communion in the direction of a hierarchical and monarchical papal church. From earliest Christianity to the early Middle Ages the image and reality of the church underwent a remarkably far-reaching change.

Bibliography

T. G. Jalland, *The Church and the Papacy*, SPCK 1944
J. N. D. Kelly, *The Oxford Dictionary of Popes*, Oxford University 1986
B. J. Kidd, *The Roman Primacy to AD 461*, SPCK 1936
Peter in the New Testament, a symposium by Protestant and Roman
　　Catholic scholars, Minneapolis 1973

3. The liturgy

Liturgy as a celebration and actualization of the saving events was familiar to the first Christians from their life in Judaism. In the early church they celebrated their worship similarly – with new content. Some liturgical elements (reading of biblical texts, homily, prayer, hymns) in earliest Christianity go back to Jewish worship. A number of liturgical texts (e.g. I Cor.11.23–25; Phil.2.6–11), rites (e.g. James 5.14–16) and concepts already appear in the New Testament. There is more abundant evidence from the early (Didache) and later (Justin, *Apology* I) second century and the beginning of the third (Hippolytus, *Apostolic Tradition*); for example, they hand down old eucharistic prayers. The liturgy was one of the spheres of life in the early church which developed with particularly marked spontaneity, originality and variation. For all their consistency in basic form, the liturgical forms differed widely in particular churches and periods. From the fourth century on, different basic types of liturgy developed in the spheres of the most significant churches (Alexandria, Antioch, Rome, Constantinople, Jerusalem and Milan), each again with local peculiarities. From the sixth and seventh centuries, for political reasons this varied picture of an unusually rich, creative and vital liturgical life in the early church was subjected to measures to unify it, on the one hand from Rome and on the other from Constantinople.

　　The leading motives of the liturgy were the commemoration of the crucified and risen Jesus, the notion of the presence of his salvation in a mystery which was performed dramatically, the longing for a participation in heavenly worship by anticipating it in the earthly sphere, the need for religious festivals, symbols and a rhythm of life generally, and in particular the experience of the faith community. In the early church the liturgy was also often related to dogma in a direct reciprocal way: it reflected and influenced the theology of the churches.

The Christians of the early period were conscious that as spiritual, inward worship, their worship differed from the pagan cult with its material use of sacrifices and so on. In fact the Christian liturgy also had marked external differences: the pagans did not see any temples, altars and images among Christians and therefore could not regard Christianity as a pious religion. Christians allowed the objection; they had community rooms (house churches) and not sacral, consecrated temples; their tables for the eucharist had neither the form nor the function of altars; and only from the third century on were there pictorial representations in the liturgical sphere; those who presided at the liturgical festivals, bishops and presbyters, were also deliberately not called priests, to distinguish them from paganism. In the first and second centuries the distinctive features of Christianity were also clearly recognizable for contemporaries specifically in the sphere of the cultic worship of God. But in the course of the third century these distinctions became unimportant to a Christianity which in the meanwhile had become markedly assimilated to its environment, and in the fourth century they were not evident at all.

The following account concentrates on sacramental liturgical actions in the later sense. Granted, the early church did not yet have any concept of the sacrament as an umbrella concept for specific liturgical actions, nor any precise theological demarcation of what were later to be called 'sacraments' from other church rites or symbolic actions. But baptism and eucharist (and penance) were a lasting theme, a lasting practice of central importance. The Greek church preferred the term *mysterion* in a very wide sense for the central saving event and for its liturgical celebration, the Latin church (after Tertullian) the word *sacramentum*. This indicated that a hidden saving action was taking place mysteriously under the liturgical sign. Here the presence and effect of salvation in the sign had not yet been explained theologically in more detail. It was Augustine (354–430) who by distinguishing between sign, invisible reality and saving event, and the disposition of the giver and the receiver, made the necessary dogmatic clarifications and thus prepared the way for mediaeval sacramental theology. Only in the twelfth century did the specific number of seven sacraments become established, as opposed to the wider concept of *mysterion* or *sacramentum* in the early church.

(a) Baptism

From the beginning, baptism as immersion in water and as washing was the rite of admission, acceptance or initiation into Christianity. And already in the earliest period what it was to be a Christian was explained in terms of this sign of the baptismal bath (e.g. Rom.6.3–5; John 3.5). At the time of the rise of Christianity there was a baptist movement in Judaism which performed a baptism of immersion as a sign of the individual's penitence and inner purification. John the Baptist is a witness to this. The earliest community may have taken over this sign as the initiation of the newly converted from there. But strikingly, the Greek terms *baptisma* and *baptismos* which it chose were quite unusual forms, and not current Greek. This must be understood as a deliberate distinction of Christian baptism from anything comparable. And in fact Christian baptism is something new, unprecedented, in the history of religion, though individual elements of the interpretation (like rebirth) also occur elsewhere.

Here we shall trace the history of the rite. By the beginning of the third century the rite of baptism had already developed a form with all the elements which were also essential for the future. The most important evidence of this is Hippolytus's church order (c.215). Earlier sources are the Didache (Chapter 7), Justin (*Apology* I, 61) and Tertullian (*De baptismo*). Hippolytus probably reproduces the liturgical practice of the church in Rome at the end of the second century. It may be regarded as representative and is used as a basis here, though it is certain that the baptismal liturgy, like all liturgy, differed from region to region.

The early church did not baptize as quickly as possible and as often as possible, but imposed conditions on those seeking baptism which had to be met in quite an extensive period of preparation. Those seriously wanting to be baptized were grouped as a special class and called catechumens (= 'those under instruction' or pupils). As a technical term, the Greek word was reserved for instruction in Christianity before baptism. So first of all those interested in Christianity were instructed in the church's teaching and life by teachers, later by the clergy. We know of the catechumenate from the end of the second century in the West, and rather later in the East. The catechumens were already given binding obligations: they were subject to the teaching, the ethics and the discipline of the church and already had a kind of membership in that they took some part in community life and even in parts of the liturgy of the word. At this time they were also under observation, as a test.

Those seeking baptism had to register. They were asked about the motives for their intended conversion. Furthermore, the Christians who 'introduced' them, i.e. had recruited them, had to speak for them. In addition the future catechumens had to give information about their personal status, whether they were free or slaves, married or single, and so on. Nor was their occupation unimportant. There were some occupations which the church with moral or cultic reservations felt to be imcompatible with faith and therefore also with the catechumenate (e.g. pimps, gladiators, soldiers, actors and also sculptors and teachers, because they lived on pagan belief in gods or taught it). Those recruited had to leave such professions or they were not admitted into the catechumenate. They were thus immediately confronted with the requirements and obligations of the community's morality and had to live like those who had been baptized. The early church regulated access to Christianity with great care and strictness. This included all catechumens having witnesses and guarantors (the later sponsors) who saw them through the catechumenate and guaranteed the sincerity of their desire for conversion to the church. Baptism was not to be administered unworthily, and there was to be no semi-Christianity.

In the fourth century there were different rites of admission to the catechumenate, for example the laying on of hands, making the sign of the cross on forehead or breast, the giving of salt (*datio salis*, the symbol of communion and/or of the driving out of demons). The time of instruction (catechesis) lasted two or three years, but could be shortened for the zealous. During this time the catechumens were strictly separated from the baptized in the liturgy. The old church orders with psychological and pedagogical skill provided for gradual entrance into the church. Instruction was followed by an examination of the Christian life-style of the catechumens and their reputation in the community, and if the outcome was positive, the last phase began as a direct preparation for baptism. The examination for admission provided for the rejection of individual catechumens. In the final phase daily exorcisms (the driving out of demons) were practised on the recruits in the form of conjuration formulae, the laying on of hands, breathing on them and making the sign of the cross on them, and these were also continued in the baptismal liturgy. The early church saw angels and demons as omnipresent and took them for granted. A place had to be created in the newcomers for the good Spirit of Christ. The bishop went into action as the last exorcist immediately before baptism.

At the beginning of the third century, then, there was this basic form of catechumenate before baptism, with strict regulations for admission, a fixed duration, examination and exorcism. In the new conditions of the fourth century after Constantine, when there was a mass interest in Christianity (cf. Chapter III, 2), the ritual of the catchumenate was changed. The church had an interest in stricter control of admission. The most important shift in practice was that while many people became catechumens and thus could take part in the liturgy of the word and feel that they belonged, because of the high demands made by being a Christian they did not reach baptism and remained catchumens for many years or all their lives (to the hour of their death). This state no longer, as before, involved all the obligations of Christian ethics. So now the time of fasting before Easter became the direct phase of preparation for those catechumens who in fact registered for baptism out of the crowd.

This registration was a separate ceremony in the presence of the bishop and sponsors and took the form of enlisting by giving one's name; the catechumenate had sunk to a lesser (permanent) state of being a Christian. By registering, Christians seeking baptism left this state and in the different churches were given a Greek or Latin designation of their own, as either the 'enlightened' (*photizomenoi*) or elect (*electi*) or 'postulants' (*competentes*). Their pre-Easter preparation for baptism consisted in penitential exercises, exorcisms and instruction. In an intensive course of forty days they were introduced to the teaching, spirituality and life-style of Christianity. The content of the teaching included the whole Bible (as salvation history), and the interpretation of the confession of faith (the *symbolum*). The wording of the *symbolum* was given to those seeking baptism only towards the end of the period of fasting, so to speak as the inner 'sanctuary' of faith and conversion (*traditio symboli*); up to that point they did not know it officially. Every recruit had to be able to say it to the bishop on the day before baptism (*redditio symboli*). During this time there were introductions to ritual, increasing in intensity until the day of baptism finally came.

Thus people were now accepted into the church in three stages: through catechumenate, photizomenate and baptism. After baptism, in Easter week, there then followed instruction on the mysteries of baptism and eucharist (mystagogy), as we know from the sermons of Cyril of Jerusalem from the fourth century. In the third century in the West the celebration of baptism itself consisted of three parts: the baptismal bath with the rites framing it, the laying on of hands and anointing of the forehead, and the baptismal eucharist.

According to Hippolytus, the bishop, two presbyters and three deacons were involved. From the third century on baptism took place in a separate cultic space (the baptismal church or baptistery); the community was elsewhere. Those to be baptized assembled by night with prayer and catchesis. The bishop exorcised them a last time and sealed them (pre-baptismal rites). Then a prayer was spoken, the oil to be used in the baptism was consecrated, and a renunciation of the devil was pronounced by those to be baptized. In the meantime they had taken off their clothes; their whole bodies were then anointed with the oil of exorcism and they were led naked into the water of baptism. While they gave a threefold answer ('I believe') to a threefold baptismal question ('Do you believe in God the almighty Father – in Christ Jesus, God's Son – and in the Holy Spirit, the holy church and the resurrection of the body?'), they were immersed three times and thus solemnly baptized. The baptismal formula proper ('I baptize you . . .') is not mentioned in the relevant sources. The sign of the baptismal bath symbolized the forgiveness of sins as purification, being buried with Christ, rising or rebirth to new life. Then followed two post-baptismal anointings with oil which represented the relationship with Christ and the giving of the Spirit. The baptismal action ended with the laying on of hands and anointig of the forehead as the communication of the Spirit by the bishop. There then followed the baptismal eucharist where the community were gathered, in which the newly baptized now joined. This eucharist was part of the baptismal liturgy. The baptismal candidates had brought food with them; as well as bread and wine this also included milk, honey and water, each with its own symbolic value (bread and wine for the eucharist, milk and honey for the fullness of salvation in the 'promised land'; water for the inner cleansing that had already taken place). Hippolytus ends his account by saying that with the end of the baptismal eucharist the proving of the individual new converts before God and in the church now began.

In the fourth century these basic elements of the celebration of baptism were enriched with many rites and forms, differing between Asia Minor, Antioch, Jerusalem, Egypt, Milan, Africa, Spain, Rome and so on. Individual rites, for example the renunciation of the devil, were given dramatic form, as was the putting off of clothing (of the 'old man'). There was consecration of the baptismal water to give the water the power of baptism. All this shows a symbolic and sacramental realism, in other words a pious interest in the 'tangible' things and rites and a very realistic notion of the presence and working of divine forces in them. There were further rites after baptism, like putting white garments on the newly baptized as a symbol of purity, the result of baptism. The rites of the communication of the Spirit after baptism (the laying on of hands and anointing of the forehead) became increasingly independent, and historically led to a complete separation of the celebration of baptism, introducing the development towards confirmation as a separate mystery (sacrament).

Special cases of baptism included the baptism of children not of age. Up to the end of the second century adult baptism was probably the rule (although infant baptisms in the first and second centuries cannot be ruled out). But for theological and church reasons infant baptism increased, though it remained controversial. In the fourth century by no means all Christians yet brought their children for baptism. It was only in the fifth and sixth centuries that infant baptism became generally established. Another special case was the baptism of someone who was fatally ill, for whom baptismal instruction was impossible for reasons of time and who could not wait for the official time of baptism. People in any case wanted baptism because it was not only initiation into Christianity but at the same time the forgiveness of sins and a turning to salvation and therefore necessary for all those at the point of death. In emergencies there was a shortened, simplified rite of baptism, and in certain circumstances even a lay person could baptize. If the person who had been given emergency baptism died soon after baptism, there were no objections. However, there were objections if the person recovered: such persons had been baptized in an inadequate way, not in the baptismal water but simply by having water poured over them fully clothed in bed. This was called clinical baptism, and had certain disadvantages; as a rule, for example, it excluded entry into the clerical state. Someone who had received emergency baptism had to ask for the laying on of hands by the bishop. One last special case was the so-called baptism of blood. Those whose thought was simplistic, who were convinced of the need of the rite of baptism for salvation and regarded it as irreplaceable, were anxious and uncertain about the salvation of a catechumen who became a martyr for Christianity, as yet unbaptized. The bishops and church fathers reassured them: martyrs are baptized in their blood. This baptism is preceded by a confession which expunges sins, and the promise given here was already sealed by death and not jeopardized as in the case of other Christians. So the baptism of martyrdom counted more than normal baptism and was not an emergency.

Because baptism had such a central significance for the early church, its symbolic and theological interpretation was correspondingly varied and intensive. In their sermons and interpretations of the Bible, bishops and theologians developed numerous theologies of baptism which found expression in liturgical symbolism. One clear example is the idea of a change of jurisdiction which takes place in those baptized. The devils are driven out of them and God or the Spirit takes possession of them. So baptism was also understood as a seal (*sphragis*) or stamp imprinted on them which (as in the case of soldiers) declares their allegiance: the baptized are clearly God's property. Baptism also signalizes the transition from death to life which means inner conversion, turning away from Satan with specific consequences for one's life-style. Baptism was understood as total and immediate forgiveness of all sins. At first there was no thought of further forgiveness of sins which could be repeated after baptism. So baptism was a 'unique' occurrence. But the early church was also occupied with the question of the forgiveness of sins and repentance because of subsequent negative experiences (see below, IV, 3, c). Furthermore, baptism was seen as the restoration of the primal state of human beings in salvation, i.e. of the image of God in them; indeed this image was even surpassed. God's Spirit was conveyed in baptism; it had to be protected as a great treasure which could be lost (through sin). Not least, being baptized meant belonging to the church as the community of salvation.

In baptism, people of late antiquity who resolved on Christian faith sought a new orientation for their lives. Here the ritual of initiation into Christianity played the role of manifesting this reorientation as conversion, bringing it about and interpreting it. Elements from everyday culture served as rites here: a bath, purification, anointing, a change of clothes, bodily gestures and so on. There was a good match between faith and life.

(b) The eucharist

The eucharist was the central celebration of the early Christian liturgy. As an element of the community life of the early church, it had a direct historical connection with the practice of Jesus and his disciples before Jesus' death of having a meal together. In earlier sources called 'Lord's Supper' (I Cor.11.20) and the 'breaking of the bread' (Acts 2.42, 46; 20.7; Acts of John 72, 85, 86, 87), in its earliest form, at any rate, the eucharist had the form and character of a meal. The biblical Easter stories show the apostles gathered for a meal. They knew that the dead Jesus was alive among them because they had shared a meal with him of the kind that he himself had instituted before his passion.

Initially the eucharist was celebrated in the evening (Acts 20.7), was combined with a proper meal, and together with this formed the 'Lord's Supper'; thus it was not just a symbolic meal (e.g. I Cor.11.20–22; Didache 9f.). Here (at least in some liturgies) the eucharistic elements (the blessing of bread and wine) framed this meal: the eucharistic bread was taken, broken, blessed and distributed before the proper meal, and the same happened with the eucharistic cup 'after the meal' (I Cor.11.25; Luke 22.20). There were models for this sequence of rites in Jewish meals. But the meal and the eucharist could also follow each other (Didache 9f.). The main meal was given the name *agape* – love meal (Tertullian, *Apologeticum* 39.16). The celebration took place on Sunday (the day of the resurrection). The name eucharist means thanksgiving.

The combination of eucharist and proper meal did not last long. Even in the first century the eucharist was separated from the agape, transferred from evening to morning, and combined with the liturgy of the word of God which was already celebrated in the morning; this still forms its basic structure. There were symbolic (Christ the rising sun) and practical reasons (a time outside the working day) for the morning celebration. These changes had consequences for the shape of the celebration. In the room where people met there was no longer any need for a table to eat from. Only the bishop or presbyter had a table for the symbolic bread and the one cup of the eucharist. The thanksgiving was the main event. People no longer reclined round the table for the meal but stood before God and spoke prayers over the gifts. The form of the meal was no longer as clearly dominant as it had been, but it was still there. As the 'Lord's table' or 'holy table', the bishop's table was the centre, around which all the participants stood. Finally, following the understanding of the eucharist as a sacrifice, it became the altar. As a church cult, what had begun in the private sphere (house churches) with evening meals in the course of time naturally needed greater and more public space.

In earliest Christianity the eucharist was first of all the commemoration of Jesus' death; its character as a commemoration is clear in the quotation of the so-called words of institution. Here bread and wine were consecrated to become the body and blood of Christ, as sacrificial gifts offered to God, since Jesus' death itself was understood as a sacrifice ('given for you, shed for you'). Furthermore, the eucharist was an anticipation of the eschatological feast and the common meal (*communio, koinonia*) with the present Kyrios and the believers. A new accent was added by Ignatius of Antioch at the beginning of the second century: the eucharist as an 'antidote to death', as the 'medicine of immortality' (To the Ephesians 20.2). We can see from this that at a very early stage a sacramental realism, i.e. a markedly material understanding of the eucharistic elements, developed (cf. also Paul, I Cor.11.29f.).

A detailed description of the Sunday eucharist at a time around 160 CE has been handed down by Justin, *Apology* I, 67 (ibid., 65f.: the baptismal eucharist). Here the eucharist is preceded by the liturgy of the word of God (originally independent), which consisted of long, continuous readings from the Old or the New Testament and an address from the president. There followed prayer by the whole community and the offering of the gifts (bread, wine and water), and then the prayer of thanksgiving (*eucharistia*), spoken by the president alone and freely formulated 'as much as he will'. There were as yet no books, formularies and prescriptions for the liturgy, though the celebration did have a basic outline. So here too the thanksgiving was at the centre, with the communion as a second focal point.

In Hippolytus's church order (c.215), for the first time a eucharistic prayer (i.e. thanksgiving) is handed down at full length and complete. Already at the beginning of the third century the simple but impressive prayer was introduced by the same dialogue with the community as it is today ('The Lord be with you . . . Lift up your hearts . . . Let us give thanks . . .'). The principal and typical elements here are the prayer of thanksgiving for the coming, life, suffering and death of Jesus and the eucharistic words of institution, which in the version quoted do not correspond with any of the forms of the biblical text (which already differ among themselves). After this follows the *anamnesis* (the commemoration) of the death and resurrection of Jesus, the offering of bread and cup, and the *epiclesis* (the invocation) of the Holy Spirit on the eucharistic gifts, to fill those who make communion (communion *epiclesis*) or, according to other liturgies, to turn the gifts into the flesh and blood of Christ (transformation *epiclesis*); finally, the doxology (hymn of praise) forms the conclusion. The basic outline of this eucharistic prayer has been preserved in the prayers which are used today.

The early church developed the theological interpretation of the eucharist with the help of many themes and images. There was great scope for this, since there was no dogma of the eucharist and no single overall view of it. So we find the most varied notions among the individual church fathers; however, these can be divided into two basic interpretations, depending on their understanding of the eucharistic elements of the bread and wine. On the one hand there is a very direct, realistic terminology according to which the bread 'is' the body of Christ. One eats of the body of Christ and drinks the blood of Christ; human flesh is nourished by the body and blood of Christ, and so the soul is filled with God. For example, Bishop Cyril of Jerusalem (who died in 386) asserts that the Holy Spirit transforms the elements into the body and blood of Christ; Ambrose of Milan (who died in 397) explains that the bread is consecrated by the words of Christ spoken in the liturgy transforming its nature into the body of Christ. This 'realistic' theology thought in very simple terms about the relationship between liturgical sign and reality: there is a mysterious connection between the sign and what is signified, so that the symbol *is* what is symbolized.

Another understanding of the symbolic character of liturgical rites and elements (e.g. in Clement of Alexandria at the end of the second century, Origen in the third century and Augustine in the fourth/ fifth century) explained the symbol (under Platonic influence) by saying that behind this visible world there exists the spiritual world, which shows itself in the material elements (like bread and wine). Thus the things 'show' the deeper reality, but 'are' not this reality directly. Different pictures of the world underlie this and lead to considerable differences in the understanding of the sacrament or the eucharist. In the long run sacramental realism established itself, rather than the more 'spiritualist' or symbolistic concept. It is the case with both traditions that in time the eucharist was increasingly understood and celebrated in a cultic-latreutic way, in other words less in the original sense as a community meal and more as the performance of sacred rites and as a public act of worship.

In the Western church, which was always very interested in the existential problem of sin and grace, the eucharist was understood as a recollection of the sacrifice of the cross, through which the forgiveness of sins constantly becomes effective anew. The Eastern church saw the eucharist more markedly in terms of the powers of immortality which are bestowed in this food. The expressions of the differing desires and hopes for salvation in particular churches preceded these trends.

In earliest Christianity, 'the breaking of the bread', 'the Lord's Supper' and then 'eucharist' were customary as designations for the eucharist, and for a while in the third century also *oblatio, sacrificium, prosphora* (= sacrifice). The word 'mass' used today became a regular term for the eucharistic celebration only after the sixth century. *Missa* (or *dimissio*) is the term for the dismissal and farewells after a gathering, and then became the liturgical name for the closing act of worship. After various stages of development, with the loss of the original meaning of the word it became the designation for the whole eucharistic liturgy.

The history of the Christian Sunday is also connected with the eucharist. The early Christians did not have their weekly celebration of the eucharist on the Jewish festival of the Sabbath, but on Sunday. In the society of the time, from the first century CE onwards this day of the week was counted the second day of the planetary week and was named after the sun and dedicated to the sun god. It was neither a festival nor a day on which no work was done. However, for Christians it was the day of the weekly celebration of the eucharist.

This was solely because of the dating of the resurrection of Jesus to (Easter) Sunday morning.

Still, the eucharist was first of all celebrated on Sunday evening, and only later in the morning (see above); from the beginning it was part of the Christian celebration of Sunday as the day of the resurrection. Of course the pagan name 'Sunday' was not intrinsically without significance for Christians. They found new names, for example the new term 'Lord's Day' (Rev.1.10; Didache 14.1, etc.), which has been preserved in many languages (especially the Slavonic and Romance languages); it was also customary to call it the 'eighth day' as the symbol of perfection and a departure from the course of time (the seven-day week) into the beyond; or even the first day (Mark 16.2; John 20.9). For Christians the week now began with this day. But even the name 'Sunday' could take on Christian significance because Christ was called the sun, and the 'first day' of creation saw the creation of life. So 'Sunday' was kept in Germanic and Anglo-Saxon languages.

In 321 Constantine introduced Sunday as a weekly day of rest for the society which he had Christianized as part of his religious policy, and on it no work was done. The institution was meant to have religious and cultic significance. But there was no Christian basis for the cultic rest from work. So reference was made to the Old Testament, and the rest from work on the Christian Sunday was derived from the Jewish sabbath commandment, with which Sunday intrinsically had no connection. By the sixth century Sunday and Sabbath had been identified completely. So the present-day Sunday ultimately arises out of the Christian Lord's Day or day of resurrection through the state legislation of late antiquity.

The topic of Sunday brings us to the question how frequently the eucharist was celebrated and how obligatory it was. The community was fully present as far as possible. But already in the first century there are admonitions against absence from worship for want of zeal (Heb.10.25), and in the fourth century this led to church regulations. Initially the celebration took place only on Sunday (Acts 20.7). The Didache and Justin describe Sunday as the day of the eucharist. To

Sunday were then added the festivals which fell in the week and celebrations after the high feasts (e.g. Easter week), along with the day of preparation for such feasts. Moreover individual local churches had their own feasts of martyrs. As a result of certain liturgical traditions (station days), in the fourth century celebration of the eucharist also spread to Wednesday and Friday (and in the East also to Saturday). So the daily celebration of the eucharist was not customary in the early church before the fourth century. At the end of the fourth century it is seen as the customary practice by many church fathers (for example Jerome, Ambrose, Augustine) and synods, so it was introduced during this century. The frequency of the eucharist must be distinguished from the frequency of communion. The latter was at first, surprisingly, greater: from the second century there is evidence of daily communion. It was a Christian custom to take eucharistic bread into homes (deacons brought it to those who were absent) and to eat it in the morning as the first food of the day. But in the fourth century it was taken for granted that all Christians communicated within the eucharistic liturgy. In the long run only the priest communicated. We can see how liturgical practices were subject to frequent and marked changes.

(c) Penance

Penance was an eminently theological and at the same time practical problem. The early church found itself faced with the question of the consequences of (grave) sin committed after baptism for the relationship between the church and sinners and for the sinner's prospect of salvation before God. In the early period the requirements for holiness were strict: there really could be no sin among the 'saints' (= the baptized); to contemplate forgiveness of such sin gave the impression of illegitimate indulgence. But the question of the salvation of baptized sinners became a burning issue on a large scale when during the persecutions of Christians in the third century there were many lapsed Christians who wanted to return to the church. Now a decision had to be made as to whether there was still a chance of salvation for apostates, and thus also for murderers, adulterers, and the like, and if so how; this could only consist in being received back into the church from which these grave sinners had separated themselves. The church authorities put forward very controversial views in this sphere, which was pastorally so important.

Preliminary decisions had been made here in earliest Christianity, which established two things: the unconditional obligation to holiness and at the same time the possibility of forgiveness. At one time conversion and baptism (as the forgiveness of sins) meant an absolute change of life, involving the rejection of sin and an acceptance of the holiness given by God. The new state attained in baptism was in no way compatible with new sin. So the separation of the sinner from the community was the practice of earliest Christianity (cf. I Cor.5.1–5; Matt.16.19; 18.18; John 20.23). The reason for this was the preservation of the holiness of the church and the seriousness of repentance and conversion. On the other hand, for all the seriousness of the claim to holiness, in Jesus' preaching there was an emphasis which ultimately made it impossible to abandon the sinner: God's gracious forgiveness of sins requires Christians to be ready to forgive friends and even enemies (e.g. Matt.6.12; 18.21f.; Luke 6.36). But that also had to apply to the church as a whole: it too had to be ready to forgive sin. Both a strict requirement of holiness and a readiness to forgive were the Christian duty of the community (II Cor.2.5–11). And practice was soon helped by the distinction between sins which 'lead to death' and lesser sins (I John 5.16f.).

This notion and practice also applied for the post-apostolic period and the church of the second century. Repentance in faith and active penitence were the presupposition for forgiveness. Both sin and forgiveness had been part of the everyday life of the early church. But at first there was as yet no organized church practice, i.e. there were no liturgical rites of penitence. These came into being only during the second century. Around the year 140 a layman in Rome wrote a work on the theme of penitence, the so-called *Shepherd of Hermas*, which by threatening that the world was at an end set a limit to the possibility of forgiveness and the opportunity for repentance, and announced a single, definitive last time for repentance. This work also distinguishes between different sins and groups of sinners, depending on the gravity of the offence. Such distinctions continued to play a role in penitential practice. Here we can recognize the beginnings of the concern to regulate penance and at the same time severe objections to ongoing forgiveness of sin. From the beginning, the practice of repentance was ruled out for some grave sins, namely idolatry (apostasy from the faith), murder and unchastity (adultery). Such cases were left to God.

> This selection which came about in the second century had to do with the actual gravity of these sins and a misunderstanding of Acts 15.20. Acts 15.20,29; 21.25 make the four obligations of the Mosaic law which also applied to non-Jews within Israel binding on Gentile Christians: abstention from idolatry, from fornication, from eating food from which the blood had not been drawn, and from blood itself. Later this was no longer understood. The penultimate point was omitted and the other three obligations were interpreted in terms of the capital sins of apostasy, fornication and murder (the prohibition against eating blood became the prohibition against shedding blood).

It is important to note that sin itself meant exclusion from the community and forgiveness meant a return to the church. Prayer, fasting and alms are known as early forms of penance.

Penance developed differently in the Western and Eastern churches from the third century on. Tertullian (who died after 220) gives us relatively clear information about the West in his book on penitence (*De paenitentia*), from which a developed penitential liturgy can be recognized. According to this, sinners made a public confession of sins (*exhomologesis*) to the community, in mourning attire and with fasting, prayer and self-accusation; they also asked the community to pray for them and to receive them back. Subsequently they were excluded from worship (excommunication) and along with other penitents had to fulfil a penitential period lasting weeks or years (to be spent in fasting or prayer). Reconciliation followed the fulfilment of this condition, first through the community, but soon, in the third century, with laying on of hands by the bishop. Tertullian calls this procedure 'second penitence' (baptism being the first, *De paenitentia*, 7.1,12) or the 'last hope'. He was one of those who always found the forgiveness of sins after baptism suspect; in the end he thought it fundamentally illegitimate and went over to the rigorist schismatic church of the so-called

Montanists. From this position he criticized the penitential practice of the church as forbidden laxity, and challenged the authority of the community or the bishop to forgive sins.

Others also opposed this; in particular they expressed the strongest objections to the forgiveness of 'deadly sins'. In 217 there was a schism in Rome as a result of the controversy between Bishop Callistus (Calixtus) and Hippolytus; here Hippolytus was the rigorist and criticized the official penitential practice of the Roman community for being too tolerant. And in 251 this situation was repeated in a sharper form in Rome when the presbyter Novatian and Bishop Cornelius disagreed over the possibility and mode of accepting back Christians who had lapsed in the persecutions. This led to the formation of the rigorist separatist church of the Novatians. Significantly they called themselves the 'pure' (*katharoi*), because in principle they argued for the exclusion of sinners from the church (cf. Chapters III, 1, b; V). It existed for centuries. There were constant attempts to 'correct' the practice, but ultimately without success. For finally penitential discipline developed in the more liberal, conciliatory direction. The main reason for this was that at all times repentant sinners kept asking to be received back into the church, and bishops did not want to deny them the chance of salvation. This pressure did not harden penitential practice, but made it more open.

Cyprian of Carthage (who died in 258) decisively advanced the church's guidance of penitential practice. In his North African church he stood between two extremes: the rigorists excluded any possibility of repentance and reconciliation for the lapsed; by contrast the so-called confessors appealed to their merits in time of persecution as compensation for the failure of the lapsed and claimed the authority to receive them back into the church (see Chapter III,1, b). As bishop and 'pope' of Africa, Cyprian disputed both positions. Against the rigorists he objected that the lapsed could not be rejected in an inhuman way, but had to be healed (like the sick). And against the tolerant confessors he objected that the lapsed should be received back only on strict conditions, since they were in grave sin: they could be saved from their 'half-dead' state only by corresponding action. So Cyprian basically pleaded for clemency, but insisted vigorously on a strict and orderly church penitential practice which through the confession of sins (*exhomologesis*) and the performance of penance led to reconciliation through the laying on of hands by the bishop, who alone had the authority to achieve this. Here Cyprian brought two things firmly and finally together: the forgiveness of sins by God and the penitential procedure imposed by the bishop in the church. Forgiveness is bound up with the procedure, and the procedure results in forgiveness. Thus church penance became a matter of episcopal authority.

Soon, throughout the West bishops were regarded as the dispensers of penance in Christ's place. From the third century, the basic outline of penitential practice as it is known from Tertullian was relatively uniform. The individual steps (*exhomologesis*, penance, reconciliation) took the form of public liturgical acts of the church, since the holiness of the community, and not just that of the individual sinner, was affected by sin. Penance was the penance of excommunication; in other words, it began with the separation of sinners from the community and their being put in the state of penitents (*ordo paenitentium*). A long road of heavy penances led back to the church. Excommunication had visible consequences and forms; penitents might not take part in the liturgy, or were allowed only into parts of it. As those who had been baptized, they were not completely excluded from it, but they had to be right at the back of the church or in the porch. They might not communicate or offer gifts, and thus remained passive and to this degree 'outside'. On the other hand they had to make an appearance, because as a help towards their penitence, throughout the penitential period at every service they received a special blessing from the bishop. At the end of the penitential period reconciliation (with prayer and the laying on of hands) signified the remission of sins, the communication of grace and a return to the community. For 'deadly sins' there was only one forgiveness. The length of the penitential period depended on the bishop or the local rules. As things developed, penitential periods were laid down for all penances. In the fifth century the pre-Easter fast was regarded as the real period of penance (and already as the period of preparation for baptism: see above, IV, 3, a). It began on the Monday after the first Sunday in Lent, but from the seventh century on Ash Wednesday, whence derives the imposition of ashes, which together with penitential garb was part of the rite.

However, this public penance was imposed only for grave sins. Thus the bishops warned against trivializing 'everyday' sins: anything that is sinful brings about a fatal separation from God. All are sinners, and penitence is the lifelong task of Christians. Penitential practice filled this pastoral 'gap'; another, private, form of penitence became established alongside public penance – but only in the sixth century. Lesser sins were confessed and forgiven without becoming a public matter in the church, without liturgical rites in the community, and even without the imposition of a severe public penitential discipline. This was the origin of so-called private confession. It took place first of all in the priest's home, from around 1000 CE in church, and only towards the end of the Middle Ages in the now customary confessional.

In the Greek East, too, penance was bound up with the church's ministry and the forgiveness of sins by God in the church's act of forgiveness. By around 400 there were penitential priests here to whom the bishops transferred the imposition of penances. But in the Eastern church, nevertheless the ministers were not ultimately those solely responsible for imposing penance, as in the West. Penitence was seen less as a matter of church discipline than as an inner process, spiritual progress in the Christian's striving for perfection. Therefore spiritual direction, to help people out of their entanglement in sin, played the dominant role in the understanding and practice of penitence. Perfect Christians were responsible for the imposition of penance, for forgiveness and reconciliation. This is particularly marked in the Alexandrian theologians Clement (died before 215) and Origen (died 254). The bishop has the authority to forgive sins to the degree that he himself has been spiritually and morally tested, but not if he lags behind. Because penitence as an educational process renews life, purifies the soul, improves people and furthers their ascent to God, responsibility for it lies with the Christian teacher and guide of souls. Baptism, public penance before the community, or alms, love, a readiness to forgive, and martyrdom are ways or means of conversion. All Christians, including the perfect, need penitence, because all are sinful. The episcopate in the East sometimes found it more difficult to establish this spiritual and pedagogical understanding of penance, with its claim to authority over penance, than did bishops in the West.

The typically Eastern notion of penance became particularly significant in Eastern monasticism. The strict earnestness with which the monk saw every sin as a 'deadly sin' led to a basic mood of sorrow over one's own failure. The experienced monastic leader guided monks through a life of penitence towards ever greater perfection. For this, new practices of spiritual progress were employed: frequent self-examination was practised, daily confession, intercession and control by brother monks; sins were forgiven by the confessor. And because the life of a monk as a way to wisdom and perfection also seemed to wider circles of the church attractive and worth imitating, these practices in the treatment of sin had their effect on the whole church. The direction of souls, intercession and blessing by the spiritual masters became more popular than disciplinary absolution by ministers. In the Byzantine church, the monks played the major role in penance; they also had authority to impose penances.

In the East at a very early stage the idea developed that guilt and punishment, sin and the duration of penance, must have an appropriate and fair relationship to each other. So in the course of the third and fourth centuries a divided or gradated practice of penance was introduced. In the form of the four so-called stages of penitence, this provided for different lengths of penance and a gradual return of the penitent to the community. This form of penance never existed in the Western church. The individual stages of penance had to be undergone in succession; they had the following designations and characteristics. 1. The 'weepers': at this stage the penitents could only enter the porch of the church, where they confessed to those arriving for the liturgy the sins which separated them from the church, and with lamentation ('weeping') asked them for their intercessions. 2. The 'hearers': at this stage the penitents were already standing at the back of the church, along with the still-unbaptized catechumens. In the Eastern church the penitents were put on roughly the same level as the unbaptized, because as a result of their sin they had lapsed from their baptism; 'hearers' was a term which in some places was applied to catechumens in the early stage of the catechumenate. 3. The 'kneelers': in this state the penitents already came up the church for some parts of the liturgy, but as a sign of their penitence had to remain kneeling. In principle, kneeling was not the liturgical custom in Sunday worship, and in the whole period from Easter to Pentecost: as the redeemed, people stood upright. Kneeling, they received a special blessing at the end of the liturgy. 4. The 'bystanders': in this last phase the penitents again took part in the whole service, standing, though they were still excluded from offering gifts and from communion.

So there was a liturgical ritual which on the one hand demonstrated the distance of the sinner from the community, but on the other tangibly represented a gradual, controlled, gradated readmission. At the close of the fourth stage the penitents were again admitted to the eucharist.

The duration of the individual stages of penance depended on the severity of the sins and was laid down in penitential canons, some examples of which we know from the penitential letters of bishops of the third and fourth centuries. According to what is said by Basil of Caesarea (who died in 379), the penitential period for murder, for example, lasted for twenty years in all (individual stages lasted for different periods of between four and seven years); for adultery fifteen years; for theft, one or two years, and so on. For 'denial of Christ' (apostasy) one remained a 'weeper' for life. However, earnest penitence could reduce the period; indeed, it is said that earnestness is more important than duration. But there were norms imposed by the church (penitential canons) and a prevailing practice, inculcated, for example, by the Second Ecumenical Council at Constantinople in 381. Apart from apostasy from faith, it also covered the capital sins which were formerly excluded from penance (murder, adultery).

This penitential practice became anachronistic as a result of the changes made after Constantine. From the end of the fourth century, the long periods of excommunication were incompatible with the new interest of the state, that every citizen should be integrated into the religion of the empire and the state. So exclusion from the church had quite new consequences, and now also had consequences in the social sphere. Offences against the ideal of holiness and the discipline of the church were at the same time a violation of public social standards, a failure over the demands of social conformity. Excommunication from the church was in the long run tantamount to social contempt. The public confession of sins before the commumity could cost people their professions, dignity and status in the realms of the state and society, and in some circumstances (e.g. murder and the like) could have consequences under criminal law. Church and society were no longer separated.

So here too the result was a privatization of the practice of penance, a secret, private confession of sins. The rites of control and separation between holiness and sin in the church shrank into mere remnants. As a consequence, 'confession' today does not denote the public and liturgical action of the church as represented by penance in the early church.

Thus in the face of rigoristic protests the early church established the authority to impose penance and the possibility of forgiveness even for grave sins, both driven by pastoral practice. It also emphasized that the theological duty of the community, the church, and Christians (including the church in its official actions) was to imitate God's readiness to forgive (instead of imposing censorious strictness) and communicate it symbolically.

Bibliography

General

J. G. Davies (ed.), *A New Dictionary of Liturgy and Worship*, SCM Press 1986

Joseph Martos, *Doors to the Sacred. A Historical Introduction to Sacraments in the Christian Church*, SCM Press and Doubleday 1981

W. Rordorf, *Sunday. The History of the Day of Rest and Worship in the Earliest Christian Church*, SCM Press 1968

Baptism

Joachim Jeremias, *Infant Baptism in the First Four Centuries*, SCM Press and Westminster Press 1962

Burkhard Neunheuser, *Baptism and Confirmation*, Herder and Herder 1964

E. C. Whitaker, *Documents of the Baptismal Liturgy*, SPCK 1960

Eucharist

Lucien Deiss, *Early Sources of the Liturgy*, Alba House 1967

Gregory Dix, *The Shape of the Liturgy*, A.& C.Black 1945

Edward Kilmartin, *The Eucharist in the Primitive Church*, Prentice Hall 1965

Theodore Klauser, *A Short History of the Western Liturgy*, Oxford University Press 1969

Penance

S. L. Greenslade, *Shepherding the Flock*, SCM Press 1967

Bernhard Poschmann, *Penance and the Anointing of the Sick*, Herder and Herder 1964

Edward Schillebeeckx (ed.), *Sacramental Reconciliation*, Herder and Herder 1971

4. Forms of piety and holiness

In every era, Christian piety has sought ways to realize faith and attain holiness. Here it has always been important for the guiding ideal to have a concrete form. Of course this was never more evident than in the life of ideal Christians, though at the same time they were venerated as unattainable heroes, because they towered so much above the average. For the first centuries it was the martyrs (both men and women) who realized the postulates of the Bible and early Christianity like 'discipleship' and 'imitation' of Jesus, almost literally. They showed the way, yet in their perfection and their fate they were a model which was almost unattainable for most people. Thus the veneration (not the imitation) of the martyr who had become so close to Christ and christlike became the concrete form in which many Christians acknowledged the Christian ideal. Other needs like those for the intercession, power and support of a helper also played a role. From the later second century the cult of the martyrs was practised in the church, both in the liturgy and in forms of private devotion. Cultic practices at the tombs of martyrs and on the days of their deaths were particularly popular, and they were borrowed or contributed from religious practices of the cult of the dead in the pagan environment. Through popular religion people assured themselves of mediators towards God, and each community began to favour a particular guardian patron and moreover to emphasize his or her physical remains (= relics) and venerate them in the cult.

What began with the figure of the martyr was transferred to prominent, holy church leaders (bishops) and ascetics (monks), i.e. to other ideal Christians. The veneration of saints was an important element of popular piety and liturgy in the early church. The spirituality of the Bible and earliest Christianity, but also much magic and superstition derived from the pagan view of the world, lived on in its private forms.

Within church life piety concentrated very narrowly on the sacraments (i.e. on eucharist and baptism) as the elements of Christian salvation. And with the support of the bishops a strange aura surrounded this central sphere of the Christian cult. In the midst of an era of the public recognition of Christianity, in which it became a monopoly, Christians resorted to the earlier practice of the 'arcane discipline': i.e., they kept the mysteries of the cult secret from unbelievers and the unworthy; only initiates might know of them, see them and taste them. The eucharistic and baptismal liturgies came under this attitude of secrecy, as did holy texts like the creed and the Lord's Prayer, and also cultic books, vessels and formulae. The significance of this measure, which in the fourth century was intrinsically anachronistic and almost impossible to implement, was that it kept baptized Christians vividly aware of the advantages of their participation in the means of salvation, and probably even more that it intensified the attractiveness and the value of the mysteries among those who were still unbaptized, and aroused their curiosity and expectation. So at this time the purpose of the arcane discipline was purely psychological and pedagogical. Thus it is an indication of the piety of the time, with its interest in mysticism and mysteries.

A quite different side of the practical piety of large numbers of church people was their social activity. The ancient sources often stress that it was the way of simple Christians to bear witness to their faith in a 'non-verbal' way. Care for the poor, the visiting of prisoners, social services within and outside the communities to widows, the sick, orphans, the needy was part of the everyday life of the church also in the period after Constantine. Mention is also often made of the social practice of a renunciation of retribution, a readiness for peace, and non-violence. The pagans repeatedly noted all this, in mockery or with appreciation, as a striking mark and typical pattern of Christian behaviour.

As early as the early second century, asceticism (a renunciation of possessions, marriage, culture, comfort, food, drink, sleep, etc), very varied forms of which were practised in the non-Christian environment, was also chosen by Christians as a form of discipleship of Jesus. It had already had a notable Christian tradition when at the end of the third century in Egypt it was developed by the hermit Antony (died 356) into monasticism as a new form of Christian existence. This impulse met with a great response in Egypt, Palestine, Syria and other countries. Pachomius (who died in 346) founded a communal form of monasticism instead of the solitary monastic life. This new development was also connected with conditions under Constantine, when many Christians were looking for serious, uncompromising forms of Christianity which they did not find in the imperial church. Monastic rules and descriptions of the lives of holy desert fathers stimulated the pious imagination far beyond monasticism and encouraged committed forms of life. Now the monks replaced the martyrs as the great models. Basil of Caesarea (died 378) made a decisive contribution here in forging a theological, spiritual and legal bond between monasticism, which had grown up spontaneously as a movement, and the church, and in establishing its structures. The Western church took up this phenomenon of the Eastern church, 'studied' it both in literature and in practice, and adopted it in a number of independent Western forms (above all Cassian, Martin of Tours, Augustine and Benedict).

These three groups – the martyrs, the bishops and the monks – were crucial as models for the piety and spirituality of the early church. They formed the elite from which the people took their guidelines. Their lives demonstrated ideal Christianity, the power of faith, the reward for toil. They were the goal towards which everyone strove. They lived in a way others sought to attain, with steadfastness and faithfulness. Their heroic action could be translated into the everyday virtues which the ordinary Christian also practised. They were the helpful intercessors and reliable guarantors of an invisible comforting truth for all.

Bibliography

Peter Brown, *The Cult of the Saints*, SCM Press 1981
D. J. Chitty, *The Desert a City*, Blackwell 1966
Bernard McGinn, John Meyendorff and Jean Leclercq, *Christian Spirituality I. Origins to the Twelfth Century*, Crossroad Publishing Co and SCM Press 1989
Helen Waddell, *The Desert Fathers*, Collins Fontana 1962

V

Conflicts, Heresies and Schisms

Church history not only led to success and unity; it was also the history of numerous conflicts and losses by which the practice and theology of the church were definitively stamped over the long term. Christianity first came into conflict with the synagogue or Judaism (see Chapters I, 2, 3 and II, 1). The confrontation with society and the state was of another kind (see Chapter III, 1). The way in which Christianity differed in its religious practices, notions and claims provoked hostility in society to its novelty, strangeness and totalitarian claim. These conflicts led to public controversies between pagans and Christians at a popular and also at an intellectual level. There was polemical discussion of images of God and understandings of the world, pagan philosophy and culture (see Chapter VII). The pagans were basically concerned to assert the old religion and its social functions against Christian deviation and rivalry. And here once again we should recall the suspicion that Christians were disloyal, and the repeated action of the organs of state against their refusal to take part in state worship and to prove their loyalty (III, 1). In the period before Constantine the relationship of Christianity to its environment was necessarily in principle and continuously burdened with the pressure to defend itself and to demarcate itself.

For the church as an institution with clear autonomy and a precise understanding of its own sphere of competence, conflicts of a new kind broke out when in the period of the imperial church claims were made by the emperors, who had meanwhile become Christian, that the state had competence over areas of Christianity, since it was the religion of the state or society. These claims were compellingly derived from the ruler ideology and the Roman understanding of religion and politics, and had always been valid in Roman religion.

Christianity, which had adopted the political and social role of the old religion, had to reject them in their traditional form. There were conflicts in which the church sought to defend its freedom and power to act over against the state (see Chapter III, 2, d).

The conflicts with which the church had to live also included internal clashes within Christianity over discipline and true doctrine or the right creed. These disputes were waged as a battle between orthodoxy and heresy. From earliest Christianity onwards, in every century there was a usually uncompromising and unsparing dispute in which some Christians disputed that others had the right faith. From the beginning teaching, as binding doctrine, played an increasing role. As a result of the historical phenomenon of deviations (heresies), the fixation on 'right doctrine' in the form of dogmas and formulae of faith constantly intensified. Even the early church's ideal of holiness, the Christian ethos, was caught up in doctrine, in that Christian holiness and churchly virtue were essentially seen in terms of orthodoxy. The passion with which dogmatic disputes were carried on, above all after the second century (see Chapter VII), can easily be understood from this marked fixation of Christianity on doctrine. The devastating polemic, the unprecedentedly sharp aggression, the rejection of union and reconciliation, the unscrupulous means of dealing with 'opponents' show how one-sidedly the essence of Christianity was now seen as dogma, in favour of which other Christian postulates were misused. As a result of partisanship, fanaticism and also power interests, these conflicts were so complicated as to be virtually insoluble. Because of its very different, undogmatic understanding of religion, ancient society had not previously known such disputes over faith. It was Christianity which first caused them through its central interest in the formulae of faith.

The early church regarded Gnosticism as the first dangerous heresy; this was an independent religion of redemption which probably arose at the same time as Christianity but independently of it, and reached its climax at the middle of the second century. It was based on a crudely pessimistic view of this world and human existence, explaining it in terms of a sharp dualism. This world is the product of an inferior god; as the result of a catastrophe which took place in the upper, authentic world (of light) this god created the material cosmos, a disastrous sphere. Consequently, parts of the light above found their way into wretched imprisonment or were banished into matter. They are the real selves of human beings, or more precisely of those who have a pneumatic (spiritual) nature. Only they, and not all human beings, are capable of redemption. Through knowledge (gnosis) of themselves and their situation they come to a redemptive knowledge of God and thus are liberated to return to the world of the God above, who is authentic and good. There is often an account of how a redeemer (in a phantom body) has come to their aid in this world.

Gnostic religion was a remarkably pluriform movement of many groups and doctrinal systems with very different self-designations. It took the social form of religious communities but also of (philosophical) schools and magical circles; it was also taught by individuals. Some Gnostic groups borrowed biblical and Christian elements in constructing their doctrines of the world and redemption and imitated church practices, just as they borrowed much in a parasitical way from other religious and philosophical traditions to illustrate their views. As a result the church felt that they were rivals and consequently regarded them all as Christian heretics, i.e. as deviations from the Christianity of the church, which they were not. Against this 'heresy' of Gnosticism the church above all defended the identity of the God of redemption with the Creator and the goodness of the world as creation; it taught that human beings were to blame for their disastrous state as a result of sin, but that grace was universal and there for all; it also taught the christology of a real (and not phantom) incarnation, the unity of the Old and New Testaments, a controlled interpretation of the Bible and the revealed doctrine of the church against the 'inventions' of the Gnostics. Gnosticism lived on as Manichaeism, named after its founder Mani (third century), until the time of Augustine and even longer as an actual rival and temptation for many church Christians. In the battle against Gnosticism the church developed many forms and methods of polemic against heretics, which could later be used down the centuries against all heresies. But at the same time church theology, with its tradition of being a quest for religious knowledge as the way to God and salvation, was persistently influenced by Gnosticism.

The early heresies also include Montanism, which came into

being in the middle of the second century in Phrygia (in Asia Minor) and is named after its founder, Montanus. Montanus understood himself to be the paraclete from John 14.16, and had as companions the women prophets Prisca and Maximilla; he founded his own church in the imminent expectation of a new age of the Spirit which was still pending after the coming of Christ. The Montanists lived a strictly ascetic and disciplined life, enthusiastically looking forward to the new end-time; they disputed the possibility of repentance in the case of grave sin (see Chapter IV, 3, c), and saw themselves as an elite of spiritual Christians as distinct from the compromising mainstream church; they also differed from the mainstream church in constitution, liturgy and discipline, and were very successful in their mission.

With the third century, controversies of a dogmatic nature in the narrower sense began. With their talk of God (the Father), Christ and the Spirit, the Bible and tradition posed the problem of the Christian concept of God (the Trinity) and, in connection with it, that of christology. These problems dominated the scene until the sixth century; names of relevant heresies include Modalism, Monarchianism, Arianism, Nestorianism and Monophysitism (for more details see Chapter VIII). They predominantly represent the problems of the church in the East. The Western churches were certainly drawn into the debate, but their own intensive preoccupation was with the Christian view of humanity, the problems of guilt and sin, grace and the freedom of the will, and the consequences of these questions for church practice. The church of the West condemned Pelagianism as a heresy. This was the theological position of Pelagius, who at the end of the fourth century provoked the opposition of the African church in general and Augustine in particular with his understanding of humanity and grace. Coming from the ascetic tradition, Pelagius was optimistic about the moral capacity of human beings, believing that they could do what God required of them. The impairment to a capacity for doing good caused by the sin of Adam was remedied in baptism, and the freedom of human beings to decide for God was sufficiently strong. However, according to Pelagius the choice and doing of the good was supported by God's grace. In protest against him and the other Pelagians, Augustine objected that because they have inherited the sin of Adam, human beings are no longer capable of doing good; in baptism they retain a proneness towards evil and are utterly and in every respect dependent on God's grace (even in the form of a predestination to salvation and damnation). Pelagian theology was intrinsically the traditional theology, especially in Rome, but under the theological leadership of Augustine the African leaders branded it a heresy in the church and thus made Augustine's theology of grace the basis of the Western tradition.

The fact that there were heretical communities led to further conflicts in everyday church practice. In the dispute over the baptism of heretics in the middle of the third century, the bishops of Rome and Africa did not agree how converts from heresy were to be treated when they came over to the Catholic church. It was the tradition in Africa and almost all over the East that in this case they should be baptized; in other words, those who had been baptized in the heretical community were treated as though they had not been baptized. This was explained theologically with the argument that anyone who (as a heretic) does not possess the Spirit cannot communicate the Spirit (in baptism). By contrast, in Rome it was the custom not to baptize (or rebaptize) converts on the assumption that they had been baptized with the right baptismal formula and thus validly. A distinction was made: the baptism was valid, but not effective. Therefore the baptism received in heresy was made effective by laying on of hands from the bishop. Those who came over to the church from heretical movements were thus treated like penitents (being received back with the laying on of hands). In 255–257 there was a conflict because Bishop Stephen of Rome (254–257) wanted to compel the African church to adopt the Roman practice (cf. Chapters III, 1, b; IV, 2, c). The Africans (led by Cyprian) and other particular churches opposed this, while for example Alexandria agreed with Rome. In the long run the Roman practice and idea of the sacrament became established: the validity of the sacrament is not dependent on the 'holiness' of the one administering it (i.e. on whether he is heretic or sinner).

In addition to the heresies there were numerous schisms in the time of the early church. Schism (division) is distinguished from heresy as involving differences in the practice and order of the

church rather than in doctrine. But the unity of the church actually
came to be lost despite agreement over dogma. The dispute over
Easter is an early example of this. The issue was the date of the
festival. At the end of the second century, almost all particular
churches celebrated Easter on the Sunday after the spring full moon,
but in some areas of Asia Minor and Syria the Christian Easter was
celebrated on the day of the Jewish feast of Passover, i.e. 14 Nisan
(hence the name Quartodecimans – those celebrating on the
fourteenth). Probably different traditions had come down from
Jewish Christianity and Gentile Christianity. Shortly after 150 there
was a discussion of the issue in Rome between Bishop Anicetus of
Rome (155–166) and Bishop Polycarp of Smyrna. No solution was
found because neither side was ready to give up its own liturgical
custom in favour of the other and for the sake of unity, nor did it see
any reason to do so. It was almost the rule that such negotiations
were fruitless. But what is untypical here is that the unity of the
church was explicitly preserved, despite the difference in the liturgy,
and although the Jewish-Christian celebration of Easter was
burdened with the suspicion that it had not been distinguished
clearly enough from Judaism. So whereas at first people did not see
any divisive schism here, the climate became much harsher when in
an ultimatum Bishop Victor I of Rome (189–199) called on the
minority churches under threat of excommunication to follow the
Sunday practice of the Roman church and most other churches.
However, the Quartodecimans were excommunicated only at the
First Ecumenical Council in Nicaea (325).

Penitential discipline became the occasion for another very
wearisome schism in the West (see Chapter IV, 3, c). In the middle
of the third century the Roman presbyter Novatian had called for the
lifelong excommunication of those who had lapsed in the persecutions, against the African church and against the majority of the
Roman community. With his followers he founded a schismatic
church (Novatians), which understood itself as the 'community of
the saints', who called themselves the 'pure' (Greek *katharoi*, hence
the later Cathars), made lofty claims for themselves and despised the
mainstream church for its laxity. They spread widely. Dogmatically
(i.e. in trinitarian theology, which was disputed at the time) they
agreed fully with the catholic church. In the fourth and fifth

centuries the emperors enacted laws against the Novatian schismatics (for the sake of the unity of the empire).

The rise and history of Donatism was a particularly dramatic development (see Chapter III, 1, b and III, 2, d), which must also be called a schism. The scene was again Africa. In Carthage a foreign bishop had taken part in the consecration of Caecilian as bishop (probably in 311/312). In accordance with the radical African tradition this consecrating bishop had been accused and disqualified as a so-called *traditor codicum*, i.e. one who had handed over the holy books or vessels to the Gentiles in the Diocletian persecution of Christians. He was thus a sinner, and (in the African view) could not perform any sacred actions, so Caecilian's consecration was not valid. An anti-bishop, Majorinus, was elected; his successor was Donatus, whose schismatic supporters were given the name Donatists. The background to the division went far beyond this occasion: the Donatists claimed to be the true church of the martyrs because of their rigorism and because they alone realized the strict ideal of holiness. This was a battle waged by a wing of the African church which advanced the radical thesis that the holiness of the minister was the presupposition for the performance of the sacrament. The drama and extent of this schism can be understood only against the background of complicated religious and social tensions in Africa, which gave the conflict its harsh forms. Constantine, who had only recently become emperor of the West, sought agreement at two synods (which in his view were two arbitrations), in Rome (313) and Arles (314). Agreement was not reached, and on both occasions the Donatists were declared the guilty parties. As a result their opposition hardened, especially as imperial support of the catholic church increased (financially and in other respects), and the Donatists themselves were subjected to police measures and official restrictions. There were violent battles over the possession of church buildings, attacks on both sides and continual state sanctions in favour of the 'catholics'; as a result the Donatists' feeling of being martyrs increased, and many people were driven over to the Donatists out of political, nationalistic and social opposition to the Roman regime. There were armed disputes with rebellious agricultural workers (who had joined the Donatists; they were called Circumcellions); the latter combined social resistance to the Roman landowners with religious support for the Donatists, who were also being put at a disadvantage by the state. The Donatist church was numerically larger than the catholic church in Africa. At the end of the fourth century Augustine, as bishop of Hippo, wanted to put an end to the aggressive disputes through conversations. When these religious conversations did not result in any agreement, a harsh state policy began. Now the Donatists were officially no longer regarded as schismatics but as heretics, so that they came under the existing laws against heretics and the sanctions provided for in them. Nor did that bring a solution. This schism (which largely remained limited to Africa) was ended when in 430 the Vandals exterminated the whole of Christianity in this stretch of North Africa (from Morocco to Tunisia). So in terms of theological content the issue was again that of the church and its holiness, and therefore the question of the efficacy of the sacrament if the moral quality of the one administering it was deficient. The debate over Donatism led to clarification: the efficacy of the sacrament is independent of the moral quality of the one administering it. What began here as schism nevertheless did have a connection with dogmatic dissent. Augustine's anti-Donatist writings became decisive contributions to the later sacramental theology of the Western Latin church.

All in all, the controversies over the orthodoxy and unity of the church were as a rule carried on with bitter harshness, in an uncompromising and polemical way. If we regard peace, unity and consensus as the criteria of Christian fellowship, the result of these disputes must be said to have been small. There were seldom formulae of union, reconciliation and reunion. But we must also speak of a history of loss, because with the loss of unity something essentially Christian was lost – in favour of the self-assertion of the particular Christianities. However, in the sphere of dogma there were clarifications and gains of great breadth and permanence.

Bibliography

Walter Bauer, *Orthodoxy and Heresy in Earliest Christianity* (1934), Fortress Press 1971 and SCM Press 1972

Peter Brown, *Religion and Society in the Age of Augustine*, Harper and Row 1972
W. H. C. Frend, *The Donatist Church*, Oxford University Press [3]1985
S. L. Greenslade, *Schism in the Early Church*, SCM Press 1952
Kurt Rudolph, *Gnosis*, T.& T.Clark 1984

VI

Theological Orientations

The early church created a wealth of theological schemes for the interpretation of Christianity. These theologies differ quite considerably from one another, depending on period, context, approach and aim, and show the breadth of possibilities for understanding Christian faith. Among the many basic theological notions of the early period there is a whole series of ideas which can be regarded in a more special sense as attempts by Christianity to find its orientation. They show its place in the history of the world generally. They define the relationship of Christianity to the non-Christian environment. And they guide individual Christians and their lives by these contexts. Such orientations corresponded to the basic needs and necessities of a very young religious community which – though it had only just come into being – was claiming total and exclusive application to all human existence, past, present and future. Many of these orientations were provoked by the objections of non-Christians to Christianity. Thus it was an apologetic answer directed 'outwards', but at the same time a confirmation and assurance directed 'inwards'.

Thus for example the question was raised how it could be that Christianity came into the world so late, if the salvation of all human beings depended on it. What about past generations, and what kind of God could have acted in this apparently arbitrary way? This and related questions made it a matter of urgency to clarify the relationship of Christianity to human history generally or to define its place in that history. The early church developed theologies of history, all of which gave the answer that God's action for human salvation did not just begin with Jesus of Nazareth but had already begun at creation, and continued in Abraham and Moses and the prophets. In Israel (some theologians thought also in Greek philosophy and in the wisdom of ancient peoples) God had always communicated himself through his Logos. God had to spend a long time preparing to lead human beings, who are weak, find things difficult to understand, and need to be educated, to the truth. As truth, Christianity had therefore always been in the world, and had not only just come into being. But only now was the truth present in complete clarity, and only now had the redemption that had been announced really happened. The history of all human beings and religions was thus stylized as the prehistory of Christianity, which contained much error but also already contained the truth. Thus the Christian experience of newness could be reconciled with the proof from antiquity. To people of late antiquity the demonstration of the great age of Christianity was a decisive argument for its truth. This notion also indicated to individual Christians in the community their own standpoint in history as a whole. They were experiencing the time when the truth which had formerly been present in a hidden way and which had been prophesied was now being fully revealed. As witnesses to these decisive events in the history of the world and salvation they were also experiencing salvation in their lives. For them the truth of their faith was the key to history as a whole. Other gods, religions, doctrines of salvation and truth no longer troubled them.

From the beginning the Christian understanding of the Jewish Bible (the Old Testament) had been of decisive significance for this self-orientation of Christianity. It was read consistently as a book of prophecy, namely in terms of Christ. Thus it was the main landmark for the early church. The ancient book already contained the truth preached by Christianity and, line by line, was the promise of the fulfilment which had now taken place. For this reason (and also for other purposes) the interpretation of scripture was not only a permanent task of the church but also the medium by which it interpreted itself. Christianity was talked about in the language of the Bible (Jewish and Christian).

And because of course the Jewish Bible is in origin and content a Jewish, not a Christian, book, it was important for the early church to interpret it 'correctly', i.e. to read it with the appropriate method, if its 'real' statements were to be disclosed. The early church was convinced that the literal sense of the Old Testament was extremely provisional and often worthless. The theologian Origen (c.185-254) expressed as a theory what Paul (e.g. I Cor.9.9f.), all earliest Christianity, and all the later interpreters had already practised as allegory. The Bible has several levels of meaning, not only the literal (or historical) meaning but also the spiritual or allegorical and typological and moral meaning. In this theory of scriptual exegesis which governed all the Middle Ages and was held to be valid up to modern times, the decisive factor is neither the sequence nor the number of the different scriptural senses but the fact that a deeper or 'spiritual' meaning of the text was accepted alongside or 'behind' the literal one. Understood allegorically, the books of the Old Testament offered the early church practically unlimited possibilities of proving its convictions from these ancient writings. With allegory, Christian theology was taking up a method which had been developed in pre-Christian Greek philosophy (for example, in connection with Homer) and had already been applied by Jews to the Old Testament. The importance of the Bible as a basic orientation of the early church explains the great mass of commentaries on predominantly Old Testament books which were written by the church fathers.

The New Testament Bible played its role of orientation in a different way. It contains the new directly, and without the need for special interpretation. In a long process which took different courses in different places, this selection was made from the many writings of the early Christian period which were in circulation (using the criteria of great antiquity or apostolicity, nearness to the origin in content, usefulness, recognition and use in the church). The result was a canon of holy books (finally defined in the fourth century) alongside the 'Old Testament', which now in a reliable, complete and binding way contained not promise and prehistory but the 'event itself', Jesus' words and deeds and the preaching of the apostles. The early church did not have this orientation as such; it had to create it by selection and demarcation.

In the course of the church's history the occurrence of heresy and schism posed it the question of orientation on its own origin. At a later period all the different groups with their contradictory teaching claimed to originate with Jesus and the apostles. Which was right?

The question was thus one of finding a reliable orientation in past church history. The Bible by itself did not solve any disputes. In the course of the second century, when the 'mainstream church' had Gnosticism as a rival (see Chapter V), it created a clear and very useful guideline here: the truth is always guaranteed by the bishop, who goes back through an unbroken chain of bishops to an apostle (or disciple of an apostle) connected with the origins of Christianity and whose preaching is the same as that of all his predecessors in the see which he occupies. Moreover the stream of truth can be traced back to the traditions of earlier Christian teachers and presbyters who reach back to apostolic times. This fundamental orientation on tradition and apostolic sucession was formulated very clearly by Irenaeus of Lyons around the year 185 and since then has always been used when the question is one of safeguarding truth lost in the course of time or disputed. In addition, in the fourth and fifth centuries the argument from the fathers was added: in points of dispute, above all at councils, one seeks the faith of the 'fathers', i.e. the theological statements of prominent theologians of earlier times, and uses these as argument and proof. Since then the church fathers have been part of the guidelines of faith. This orientation on tradition, succession and the fathers, i.e. on the past, drew much of its probative force from the widespread pre-Christian idea in ancient thought that when it comes to the possession of truth, the early past is superior to the present. But the proof from tradition was not the whole orientation; above all it did not suppress the Bible. Rather, the Bible, the meaning of which was often disputed, was read with the tradition and with the fathers.

Bibliography

P. R. Ackroyd and C. F. Evans (eds.), *The Cambridge History of the Bible. 1. From the Beginnings to Jerome*, Cambridge University Press 1970

H. F. von Campenhausen, *The Formation of the Christian Bible*, A.& C. Black 1972

R. P. C. Hanson, *Tradition in the Early Church*, SCM Press 1962

VII

The Theological Literature of
the Early Church

A large number of Christian writings have been handed down from the period of the early church (an even larger number have been lost). They are written in Greek, Latin and various Eastern languages (e.g. Syrian, Armenian and Coptic). The production of such extensive Christian literature was no coincidence: Christianity was communicated not only as worship, but also in statements, doctrine, confessions, mission and theology. Therefore it was essentially dependent on language and linguistic communication, and thus also on the written word. As a result we have many written sources for our knowledge of the early church: the predominant content of them is the preaching of the faith, biblical exegesis, explanations of the mysteries of salvation, moral instruction, demarcation from Judaism, paganism and heresy, and expositions of the Christian creed to serve the ends of instruction, edification, recruitment or apologetics. The usual literary forms in earliest Christianity and the early Christian period are the letter, the circular letter, the gospel, the apocalypse, acts of the apostles, homilies, and in later centuries letters, speeches (sermons or apologies), tractates, commentaries, dialogue; in addition, creeds, liturgical texts, acts of martyrs, lives of monks, and acts and decisions of councils have also come down to us in written form. There follows a selection of the most important names and dates from the history of early Christian literature.

The New Testament contains the earliest extant Christian writings: Paul's First Letter to the Thessalonians (from 51/52) is the earliest Christian document. The latest parts of the New Testament were already written considerably later and come from the time around 120–130 (Jude; II Peter). The earliest Christian writing which did not find its way into the biblical canon, the so-called First Letter of Clement, written from Rome to Corinth, dates from as early as 96–98. Along with other writings from the early second century, above all the seven letters of Bishop Ignatius of Antioch, the two letters of Bishop Polycarp of Smyrna, the letter of Pseudo-Barnabas, a Second Letter of Clement, the Didache (a form of church order) and the *Shepherd of Hermas*, these are termed the Apostolic Fathers, because they were relatively close in time to the apostolic era. They were intended for use within the communities and (with the exception of the letters of Ignatius, with their original statements about the church, the monarchical episcopate, the eucharist and the theology of the martyrs) have a simple theme related to praxis: teaching, morality and order. This is explained and inculcated at a very simple level. Warnings against a lapse into paganism or Judaism or apostasy into heresy are a distinctive theme. Here (as in the late writings of the New Testament) we have a reflection of the milieu and the sphere of community interests at a later time, when stability in doctrine, morality and church order became important.

The second and third centuries saw the rise of the so-called apocryphal ('hidden') writings, only a part of which were read in the mainstream church; the rest were composed in marginal groups. They primarily satisfied pious curiosity and imagination by relating fantastic miracle stories about the childhood and resurrection of Jesus, presented entire romances about apostles or reported revelations about the end of the world, heaven and hell – largely for a popular audience. This literature was written in the earliest Christian literary forms of gospel, apostolic acts, apocalypse and letter.

The martyr-literature of the second and third centuries was aimed at the popular needs of the average church. It is about the christlike attitude of the martyrs under trial, in suffering and dying, their religious superiority to their persecutors, their unshakable loyalty, endurance and confidence in salvation. They are biased towards an edifying instruction of Christians and an encouragement of pious veneration. Accounts of trials, torture and executions have been handed down for this purpose. These writings, some of which are historical and some of which are also legendary, have also been composed as the accounts (sometimes in the form of letters) or the records of trials (acts). The earliest example is the martyrdom of Polycarp, composed shortly after the middle of the second century and usually counted among the 'Apostolic Fathers'. The Acts of the Scillitan Martyrs, an account from 180 of the martyrdom of six Christians in Carthage, is probably the earliest Christian work in Latin.

Around the middle of the second century the Greek apologists ('defenders') for the first time wrote works intended for non-Christians (pagans or Jews) and which were to be read by them. These refuted misunderstandings about Christianity and slanders against it; in other words, they rejected the objections of non-Christians, and gave information about Christianity in a way which was regarded at the time as 'reasonable', acceptable and ultimately superior. The pagan tradition (of religion and philosophy) was (at least in intention) presented so as to make readers in search of salvation feel that it let them down and that Christianity represented the answer to the questions which it failed to meet. This criticism of paganism and commendation of Christianity was primarily addressed to the educated with their typical reservations about Christianity, which they regarded as an absurd religion, one for superstitious, uneducated people. So on the one hand an effort was made at the literary level. On the other hand, the apologists paid a good deal of attention to the philosophical and religious thought of their non-Christian audience, so that Christianity as outlined in these writings can sometimes seem pale and strange. The central argument consisted in a proof that both the popular and the intellectual criticisms of Christianity were unjustified: that Christianity was not novel (and thus unqualified), but old and venerable, and indeed older than pagan religion or philosophy; that in all its individual notions of God, the world, human beings and human happiness (salvation) Christianity surpassed paganism; and that the pagan philosophers, particularly Plato, had already spoken the truth, because this had been communicated to them by the divine Logos. Finally, it was no great step from (Platonic) philosophy to Christian faith, and everyone had to take this step in a rational way. The authors of these works were Christian teachers. In the second century the most important of them is Justin (from Palestine, though he worked in Rome); the *Apologies* of Athenagoras, Aristides, Tatian and Theophilus of Antioch have also been preserved. This kind of apologetic continued until the third and fourth centuries. We cannot discover whether these works were read by non-Christians, and if so with what effect.

In the meantime, in the middle of the second century Gnosticism reached its climax (see Chapter V) and also produced an extensive literature. The Apologists also wrote against it. Around 185, Irenaeus, Bishop of Lyons, wrote his work against the Gnostics (*Adversus haereses*), in which he demonstrated the unity of God and the Bible, the chance of redemption for all people, and the church's guarantee of salvation and truth, and developed the principles of a reliable explanation of the Bible and tradition and a proof of succession (see Chapter VI).

Down to the third century the church had spoken and written in Greek, even in the West. But in the course of the third century, Latin established itself in liturgy, preaching and literature. One of the leading theologians who now formulated Christian theology in the Latin idiom was the African Tertullian (he died after 220). He was fluent in both languages, but spoke Latin. We have a series of writings from him on different topics: against the Gnostics, against the pagans and the Jews, on topics relating to church practice and morality (repentance, baptism, prayer, patience, theatre-going, marriage), and on the Trinity (*Against Praxeas*). After he had gone over to Montanism (see Chapters IV, 3, c; V) he wrote rigorist tractates on the demands of the Christian life-style and criticized the mainstream church. Two of the typical characteristics of Latin Christianity can be recognized in Tertullian: the topic of the Christian practice of faith and the clearly legalistic and disciplinary way of describing the church and Christianity.

One of the last Christians still to write Greek in the West was Hippolytus of Rome (who died in 235); he was one of the most productive writers in the early church. A rigorist, Hippolytus was involved in a schism with Callistus (Calixtus, 217–222) as anti-bishop of Rome on questions relating to the doctrines of the Trinity and penitence. He wrote a work entitled 'The Refutation of All

Heresies' (*Refutatio omnium haeresium*), which describes the heresies of church history down to his day. He also wrote *On the Antichrist* and a chronicle of the world, in order to calm down some nervous expectations in the church by providing information about the real signs and the actual date of the end of the world (he said that it was not imminent). Many of Hippolytus's works on the Bible are lost. His exposition of Daniel is the earliest Christian commentary on the Bible that we have (around 204). Hippolytus's *Apostolic Tradition*, a church order, is important for our knowledge of practice in the early Roman church.

Among Latin authors in the West, mention should also be made of Novatian, who was a prominent presbyter in Rome around 250. His most significant extant work, *On the Trinity*, is (like Tertullian's *Against Praxeas*) a testimony to the amazingly early development of trinitarian conceptuality in the West. Novatian's divergence over the question of penance and his foundation of a schismatic church (see Chapters IV, 3, c; V) did not affect his accord with the mainstream church over the dogmatic image of God (the Trinity). We have already met the African Cyprian of Carthage (who died in 258) in connection with the history of the episcopate, penance and the dispute over heretical baptism (Chapters IV, 2; IV, 3, c; V); his works *On the Unity of the Church* and *On the Lapsed*, along with a series of letters, reflect his efforts to consolidate his position. Arnobius and Lactantius, who undertook a kind of reckoning with paganism in the period when there was a change of course in religious politics between Diocletian (Galerius) and Constantine, were strange Christians. They wrote their polemic with literary skill, but with a suspect ignorance of church dogmatics. Arnobius wrote seven books *Against the Pagans* (*Adversus nationes*) with arguments which were already conventional, and above all with a proof which was topical between the second and the fifth centuries, to the effect that Christians were not to blame for the historical castastrophes of the time consisting of war, epidemics and economic crises. The content of the seven books of the *Divine Institutions* is similar, but they differ even more markedly in their depiction of the substance of Christianity. His work on *The Manner of Deaths of the Persecutors* (*De mortibus persecutorum*) describes with great satisfaction the painful but just end of all the emperors who engaged in persecution: here we have documentation of the feelings of revenge and resentment among Christians ('semi-converted' Christians) during and after the time of persecution.

The literature which was written from the late second century onwards by Christians in the city of Alexandria, one of the centres of knowledge in the ancient world, brings us into a very different atmosphere of the early church. Here Christian theology was articulated in philosophical and scientific forms of thought in order to do justice to the contemporary criteria for science and to enable it to be discussed and accepted by the educated. This was the contribution of Alexandrian teachers of Christianity, who in a deliberate missionary and apologetic effort presented Christianity in accordance with the rule of the academic schools in their city. They gave private lessons to an interested audience in Christianity as the 'true philosophy', in the same way as other teachers taught their philosophy. They are known as the Alexandrian school, a term which we must take to indicate the teaching and theology of Christian teachers (laymen), communicating Christianity in the form of free teaching, with no official responsibility. The theology of this 'school' was also written down in books. The first of the Alexandrian teachers known to us is Pantaenus (around 180), but the first literary works that we have come from Clement of Alexandria (who died around 215). We have three major works of his: the *Admonition against the Pagans* (*Protreptikos*), *The Pedagogue* (*Paidagogos*) and *The Carpets* (*Stromateis* or *Stromata*). These criticize pagan philosophy and mythology, but at the same time attempt to form links with philosophy. The Christian teacher, himself an educated man, spoke and wrote about Christ and Christianity in such a way that the interested educated non-Christian might possibly read about them. The concepts and arguments which he used were similar to or the same as those of philosophy. And with Clement of Alexandria all talk of Christianity had a 'Gnostic' dynamic; in other words, he was passionately concerned with knowledge. Clement was fond of calling Christianity the gnosis (= knowledge) which is superior to all other knowledge; and the ideal Christian is the true Gnostic. Here 'gnosis' is committed knowledge of God, to be deepened all through life on the basis of revelation; it is also a Christian life in keeping with this knowledge.

All this has esoteric features: not all Christians achieve the same (Gnostic) level.

All this is also true in principle of the writing of Origen (who died in 254). He too was a Christian teacher in Alexandria. Important parts of his gigantic literary work have been preserved. A relatively systematic treatise, the four books *De Principiis*, shows particularly clearly how Christianity was presented with the aid of Neoplatonic and also Gnostic, i.e. non-Christian, views; in this way of course it underwent changes. The same work contains the theory of the multiple senses of the biblical texts (see Chapter VI). In academic commentaries and in painstaking works of textual criticism, but also in homilies (sermons) for the ordinary person, for decades Origen was concerned with the understanding of the Bible, for himself and others, for both educated and simple Christians. And since he was directly involved in the church (more strongly than Clement), in addition to his academic works we also have more popular writings, for example the apologia *Against Celsus* (*Contra Celsum*), a pagan critic, dialogues to explain true doctrine, polemic against heretics, an 'Encouragement to Martyrdom', a work 'On Prayer' and so on. The monasticism of the fourth to sixth centuries was particularly inspired by his works on biblical exegesis in its mysticism of the ascent to God. Origen made a distinction: very few Christians have the strength and dedication to attain gnosis and perfection, and most content themselves with mere faith and a minimal morality. Because of some details of his teaching, Origen fell into discredit after his death and was repeatedly condemned by the church as a heretic.

In addition to many original, fruitful ideas and impulses in Alexandrian theology, the particularly pioneering feature of this literature is that in it Hellenistic philosophy was accepted as an interpretation of Christianity. This is a development which was quite far-reaching not only in church history but also in intellectual and cultural history. It is the encounter of Christianity and antiquity, in the form of the Hellenization of Christianity: in other words, the formulation of Christian dogma with the help of Greek concepts and thought-forms. That did not happen only in Alexandria; traces of it can already be found among the Apologists. However, the Alexandrians pursued this encounter in a way which was to be particularly influential on the later history of theology. And their

'Platonic' Christianity represents the first methodical attempt to give a rational demonstration of the possibility of Christian belief. The method of Alexandrian theology also includes its philosophical mediation of the allegorical interpretation of the Bible.

Eusebius of Caesarea (died c.339), a follower of Origen, introduced a new genre into early Christian literature when at the beginning of the fourth century he composed his *Church History*. In it he brought together a great deal of very valuable information, documents and sources, to demonstrate that with Christianity the unqualified truth had come and the zenith of all history had been reached. His enthusiastic attitude to the emperor Constantine the Great is also to be understood in terms of this euphoria. He wrote a *Life of Constantine* and also a eulogy of him, since in his view Constantine, as God's instrument, had helped the church to make a historical breakthrough (see Chapter III, 2). Eusebius's *Church History* was later continued by others, for example by Gelasius of Caesarea (died 395), Socrates (c.380–440), and rather later by Sozomen and Theodoret of Cyrrhus (died about 466).

There is a wealth of theological writings from the fourth and fifth centuries, the time of the great controversies over the theology of the Trinity and christology in the East (see Chapter VIII). Here Christian literature and contemporary theological debates were particularly closely interwoven. Athanasius (295–373), from 328 Bishop of Alexandria, is one of those who took up not only a political but also a literary position in the dogmatic dispute and thus exercised influence. He composed his *Speeches against the Arians* and wrote about the history and results of the Council of Nicaea (325) in order to establish the council and its theology (see VIII, 3, 4). Apologetic directed towards pagan and Jewish points of view was also topical in the fourth century, and Athanasius also wrote such works. Spiritually, his *Life of Antony* (see IV,4), written about 357, was very influential: it was a legendary narrative about the life of the desert fathers, and its description of the monastic ideal caused this to meet with a tremendous response in both East and West. It was one of a genre.

Like the literature of antiquity and late antiquity generally, the history of early church literature also knows the phenomena of anonymity (a work is handed down with no indication of the author, so that the author is unknown) and pseudepigraphy (the name of the author given is false, whether by mistake, through confusion or on purpose); thus the context of many works is either difficult or impossible to identify. Books were also destroyed. Heretical books, like pagan works and works hostile to Christianity (see Chapter III, 1, b), were destroyed because of their content. Hence, for example, not a single work of the controversial Arius (see Chapter VIII) has been preserved intact; we have Arius's writings only in fragments, in quotations from his opponents. And the writings of the most extreme opponents of Arianism, from the far side of the other wing (e.g. those of Marcellus of Ancyra and Eustathius of Antioch), have also been destroyed either totally or apart from a few fragments. Thus books were not only lost by chance; there were also 'organized' losses in early Christian literature.

The second half of the fourth century and the early fifth century are regarded as the hey-day of early church literature, because the writing at that time was particularly distinguished, as was its theological content. The 'classics' of this period include first and foremost the three Cappadocian Fathers, i.e. the brothers Basil of Caesarea (c.330–379) and Gregory of Nyssa (c.335–394), along with Gregory of Nazianzus (c.330–390). They all came from Cappadocia in Asia Minor and all were at some point bishops. In content their writings are part of the dogmatic controversy in the phase between the First and Second Ecumenical Councils (see Chapter VIII, 3–5). The Cappadocians produced arguments in support of the Nicene doctrine of the Trinity and made a significant contribution to the theological preparation of the Constantinopolitan Creed (381). Moreover the theological and practical contribution to asceticism and monasticism and to Christian spirituality generally which they left behind in their writings was of great influence. Anti-Arian dogmatic works by Basil have been handed down (e.g. *On the Holy Spirit*), along with ascetical writings (e.g. two monastic rules), sermons and discourses on biblical texts, other discourses, and hundreds of letters. Works by Gregory of Nazianzus worth mentioning are his dogmatic discourses, speeches and sermons on various occasions, many letters, and not least his poems. Gregory of Nyssa, theologically the most prominent of the three, also left dogmatic works, all directed against heresy, along with exegetical and ascetical writings, discourses and sermons. The quantity and quality of these works can hardly be illustrated here. Certainly their literary and oratorical quality is as important as their content and their standing in the history of dogma. The Cappadocians proved themselves the equals of pagan writers by combining the aesthetic qualities of artistic literature with the Greek culture of philosophical thought and transferring these to Christian themes. So scholars speak of the 'Christian Platonism' of these early church writers. This literature is particularly important for the way in which it interweaves Christianity with the culture of late antiquity. In another sense the Cappadocians stand in the Alexandrian tradition of Origen, Athanasius and so on. Mention should be made at this point of Cyril of Alexandria (died 444), with his exegetical and polemical writings against Nestorius (cf. Chapter VIII, 6 and 7).

Another theological and literary centre of the early church, Christian Antioch, was no less significant than Alexandria. There was a famous Antiochene school. In this case the term 'school' means a particular theological tradition with a homogeneous character. Its special character is expressed most clearly in biblical exegesis. Although they too allegorized, the Antiochene theologians had an approach with a stronger orientation on history and the wording of the Bible, while the Alexandrians practised allegorical interpretation exclusively. As a result, each tradition arrived at different schemes and options in difficult dogmatic topics, above all in christology. Conversely, it can also be said that Alexandrians and Antiochenes put different emphases on both exegesis and dogmatics. This led to endless disputes, though there were also extra-theological, church-political reasons for their vehemence. One fluent Antiochene writer was Diodore of Tarsus (died before 394), though only fragments of his works against pagans, Jews and heretics and on the Bible have survived. The reason for this was once again that later his writings fell into disrepute because in the subsequent dispute over Nestorius Diodore was 'discovered' to have been a heretic. Nestorius' teacher, the most prominent Antiochene exegete Theodore of Mopseuestia (who died in 428), met with an even harsher fate: very little of his abundant writings on the Bible have been preserved directly. The situation is more favourable with John Chrysostom (died 407), who was also an Antiochene. Many of his sermons have been handed down, along with treatises (*On Priesthood*, on education, ascetic questions and monasticism) and letters. And again, only fragments survive of the writings of Nestorius (who died after 451), condemned by the church for his christology (see Chapter VIII, 6, 7) and characterized as the arch-heretic, on the basis (as present-day scholars have shown) of misunderstanding (some of it deliberate) and unjustly. He wrote apologies, letters, treatises and sermons.

Monastic literature, written predominantly in Egypt, was a distinctive genre of early Christian writing. The monks in Egypt were occupied not only with practical asceticism but also intensively with theology and spirituality, so they also produced literature. The first monastic writer to stand out is Evagrius Ponticus (346–399), who was markedly inspired by Origen and who made Origen's theology more radical at several points. He was condemned along with Origen at the Fifth Ecumenical Council in Constantinople in 553. His significance lies above all in the sphere of asceticism, mysticism and piety, especially of monasticism. He compiled various collections of biblical sayings and sentences (doctrinal sayings) for monks and also wrote biblical commentaries. Later writers are dependent on him, like his disciple Palladius (died before 431), whose books provide information about monasticism and its ideals, and John Cassian (died about 430), who reported to the West on Eastern monastic life and wrote down numerous conversations (*collationes*) with monastic fathers. A large collection of sayings, examples and precepts of famous monks was made at the end of the fifth century; it was known as the *Apophthegmata Patrum* (*Sayings of the Fathers*). The literature about the monastic fathers in the East was partly brought to the West; it strengthened the monastic ideal there to a degree that would have been inconceivable without it.

In this period (fourth and fifth centuries) the Western church took over a good deal from the Eastern church in both form and content. Much of the historical, exegetical and dogmatic work of Eastern theologians was also translated. For example, Hilary of Poitiers (c.315–367) gained a good deal of the theological competence of his exegetical and anti-Arian writings from being banished by the emperor for some years to Asia Minor, where he came to know the current dogmatic problems and the theological schemes of the

Eastern churches at first hand. Ambrose of Milan (died 397) is another decisive figure in this reception of academic and spiritual theology from the Eastern church. In his many works on the Bible he was dependent on the Alexandrian Jew Philo (c.25 BCE to c.50 CE) and the Greek fathers, to whom he was also indebted for his access to Neoplatonic philosophy as an interpretative framework for Christian biblical exegesis and theology. Among other things, Ambrose wrote on ascetical, dogmatic and liturgical-mystagogical topics. Rufinus of Aquileia (died 410) was an almost classic example of the attitude of the Western church: he translated a whole series of texts from the Eastern church into Latin from Greek to make them accessible to the West; the works were principally those of Origen, but were also by Basil, Gregory of Nazianzus, Evagrius Ponticus, and included church histories and monastic texts. Jerome (c. 357–419/20) was also active as a translator. First, he created the majority of the so-called Vulgate, i.e. the Latin translation of the Bible which (in a new revision) is still used in the Catholic church today. He also translated the Old Testament from the Hebrew; for the Gospels in 383 he revised the existing divergent Old Latin translations, which over the centuries were then displaced by the Vulgate (the Vulgate of the letters of Paul and the Catholic Epistles seems to have been made before 410 by a translator, and not by Jerome himself). Jerome also translated texts from the Greek fathers (Origen, Eusebius, Didymus) and monastic rules. He wrote exegetical works, extremely polemical books against his dogmatic and personal opponents, a catalogue of church writers and also monastic biographies and letters. Jerome's works indicate an extraordinary degree of factual knowledge and are of high literary quality.

Christian literature of the fourth and fifth centuries also includes poetry. Gregory of Nazianzus and Ephraem the Syrian (306–373) were significant poets in the East, and poets in the Latin West included Ausonius (died after 393), Prudentius (died after 405) and Paulinus of Nola (353–431), all three from the area of Gaul and Spain. Conventional themes (e.g. the topic of Christianity and paganism, the stories of martyrs, the dispute over the soul between good and evil powers) were given poetic form.

This brief sketch can only offer an approximate survey of the works even of Augustine (354–430), the most significant theologian and writer of the Latin church in antiquity. Augustine, too, is in some respects indebted to the theology and literature of the Eastern church (though because he did not know Greek well, here he had to rely on translations). But his theological and indeed literary independence is far more significant than his dependence. From his profession as an orator, Augustine had a command of rhetoric with all its linguistic artifices, and the quality of his writings benefited quite considerably from this. The immense productivity of authors like Augustine (and Origen) was possible only because they had a number of stenographers and calligraphers at their disposal. Augustine's works were the subject of lively and controversial discussion during his lifetime and in all subsequent periods. He exercised his influence particularly through the written word.

A list of his works can begin with the thirteen books of the *Confessions* (written between 397 and 401), in which in the genre of account and interpretation, prayer and meditation, Augustine retraces in retrospect his varied life to the time when he was baptized and entered the church. Another retrospect is the *Retractations* (426–427), which Augustine composed in his old age in the style of an assessment and self-criticism, surveying all his works for his own benefit and that of his readers, giving details of the content, occasion and purpose of individual works and adding supplements or corrections. From after his conversion (in 386) to 400 Augustine wrote philosophical works on the knowledge of the truth and God (against agnosticism and scepticism), the problem of evil and the human soul. Towards the end of his life he wrote some apologetic works, namely one *On the Heresies*, another *Against the Jews*, and above all his important and extensive work *The City of God*, which he worked out gradually in twenty-two books in the years between 413 and 427. The conquest of Rome in 410 by Alaric was its specific occasion: Augustine argues against the old charge, which was being revived at that time, that the Christianizing of the empire was the cause of Rome's decline. To this end he developed his extensive theology of history, according to which the world is divided metaphysically into the city (or state) of God and the city of this world (*terrena civitas* or *civitas diaboli*), and what actually happens in history is a battle between these powers. On the individual-existential and moral level this is a conflict between humble faith and the arrogant pride of human beings before God. So history is also the drama of the acceptance and repudiation of God by human beings, and to this degree the history of salvation and damnation. Secular history is developed by Augustine within the framework of this Christian perspective: this world (including Rome) is passing away; history demonstrates the intensification of its real decay and stands under the sign of its end. The historical crisis of 410 was only one detail in this overall course and thus not the singular catastrophe which Augustine's contemporaries with their Rome ideology felt it to be. The border between the two *civitates* cannot be recognized by human beings within history. But by their relation to God, human beings determine which city they belong to. In simplified form these ideas of Augustine's (with over-simplified identifications of the *civitates*) influenced fundamental mediaeval ideas of order (e.g. those about church and state) and also Luther.

A series of dogmatic works contain explanations of the creed, discussions of marriage, the relationship between faith and action, and so on. The fifteen books of the great and demanding work *On the Trinity* (written between 399 and 419) contain Augustine's independent and original contribution to the main dogmatic problem of the fourth century (the so-called psychological doctrine of the Trinity, which explains the interaction between the three divine persons by analogy with the interplay of the spiritual powers in human beings). The great dogmatic controversies and confrontations of the time are also reflected in Augustine's writings. There are the anti-Manichaean works, in which he dissociates himself from the fundamental positions of Manichaeanism, which for some years had been his religion or world-view. These are about the problem of evil, the theological quality of the Old Testament, the correct interpretation of the Bible and the christology of the real incarnation (e.g. the books *Against the Manichaean Faustus*, 397–8). The anti-Donatist writings (see Chapter V) explain the relationship between the ideal of holiness and sin, the concept of the church and the sacraments (e.g. seven books *On Baptism against the Donatists*, 400–401; *Against the Donatist Bishop Gaudentius*, 421–2). Augustine was personally very much involved in his anti-Pelagian writings (cf. Chapter V, from 412), since here the discussion was of the tradition of the African church with its fundamental theological views on original sin, grace and human freedom, predestination and baptism (especially the baptism of infants). In 411/412 Augustine wrote the three books *On the Merits of the Sinner, the Forgiveness of Sins and Infant Baptism*, and later two books *On the Grace of Christ and Original Sin* (418); and one of his significant discussions with the intelligent Pelagian Julian of Aeclanum (who died about 454) remained unfinished because Augustine died while writing it, in 430. In these writings Augustine argued that salvation was exclusively brought about through grace, which God gives without any indebtedness to human beings, not on their merits, but purely on the basis of his free election and predetermination. For their part, human beings are so damaged in their nature through original sin and their own sin that they are incapable of the good and are constantly subject to an inherited tendency towards evil (concupiscence). The influence that Augustine exercised on the later history of theology with these ideas was so intensive and direct because they had been expressed in written form in his works. Augustine also wrote some treatises against the Arians. He also wrote extensively on biblical interpretation. The presuppositions and methods of interpreting the Bible were explained in the four books *De doctrina Christiana*, which were written between 396 and 425, giving rise to a kind of doctrine of Christian culture, because in them Augustine pursued the programme in order to utilize the benefits of ancient education for Christian study of the Bible. Interpretations of the books of the Old Testament include twelve books *On the Literal Meaning of the Book of Genesis* (401–4) and the extensive *Commentary on the Psalms* (392–420), and those on the New Testament include two books *On the Sermon on the Mount* (394) and the particularly important 124 *Treatises on the Gospel of John* (407–8). A series of works discuss moral or ascetical themes like lying, marriage and celibacy, widowhood and the monastic life. Hundreds of sermons have been preserved, as, too, have numerous letters, very different in content, length and significance. Some monastic rules are attributed to Augustine, but these come from a later period: Augustine did not write a formal rule for monastic life, but simply gave some relevant instructions (Letter 211.1–4). Augustine's works were all composed with great care, and the most difficult and most important of them were usually worked out over many years.

Two popes should also be mentioned among the Latin Christian writers. Leo I (440–461) left behind letters and sermons which document his intervention in problems of dogma, politics and church politics, as do the homilies and more than 800 letters of Gregory I (590 to 604); from the latter we also have writings on pastoral and pragmatic matters. He also wrote a very extensive instruction on moral and ascetical questions in the form of a commentary on the book of Job (*Moralia in Hiob*). A work in dialogue form tells of great saints of Italy and their miraculous lives.

So the great period of the history of early church literature was the fourth and fifth centuries. Certainly a great deal of writing continued to be produced between the sixth and the eighth centuries, but it was not of the same originality and creativity, but predominantly reproduced earlier works or offered collections of them. For example, Leontius of Byzantium (who died before 543) and the unknown Pseudo-Dionysius the Areopagite (around 500) are writers who made collections from the earlier tradition and summed it up (here, however, again showing some independence of judgment). Maximus the Confessor (c.580–662) also quite deliberately based himself on the traditions of the fathers of the third to fifth centuries. And John of Damascus (c.650 to c.754) is particularly significant with his programme of not wanting to make statements of his own, but submitting himself to the tradition of the fathers, though of course he did this in the style of his own theological and literary achievement. The period of Greek early church literature is generally thought to have ended with John of Damascus and that of Latin literature with Isidore of Seville (c.560–636), who was also historically significant in conveying tradition.

Bibliography

Berthold Altaner, *Patrology*, Nelson 1960
Peter Brown, *Augustine of Hippo*, Faber 1967
H. F. von Campenhausen, *The Fathers of the Greek Church*, A.& C. Black 1963
H. F. von Campenhausen, *The Fathers of the Latin Church*, A.& C. Black 1964

R. M. Grant, *Greek Apologists of the Second Century*, Westminster/John Knox Press and SCM Press 1988

Adalbert Hamann, *How to Read the Church Fathers*, SCM Press and Crossroad Publishing Company 1993

Johannes Quasten, *Patrology* (three volumes), Newman Press 1960

Boniface Ramsey, *Beginning to Read the Fathers*, SCM Press 1993

Wilhelm Schneemelcher, *New Testament Apocrypha* (two volumes), Westminster/John Knox Press and James Clarke 1991, 1992

Maurice Wiles, *The Christian Fathers*, SCM Press 1977

VIII

The First Four Ecumenical Councils

1. Council and ecumenical council

Of the countless councils which were held everywhere in the particular churches for a great variety of reasons from the second century on (see Chapters III, 1, b; IV, 1; IV, 2, b), in the course of history a few have been given elevated status as so-called ecumenical councils. The designation implies that such synods did not just represent a part of the church and did not merely have a local theme, but represented the whole church throughout 'the world' and passed binding regulations on matters relating to the universal church. According to a numbering which became established in the sixteenth century and was continued after that, in church history so far there have been twenty-one ecumenical councils, eight of them in the time of the early church. It is impossible to give any identifying characteristics of the ecumenical councils, as though they were all of the same distinctive type. The essential criteria for a universal council given in the past and still existing in the new church law (1983 *Code of Canon Law*, c.344) are that it should have been convened by the pope of Rome and that the topics and the agenda, the conclusion of the council and the confirmation of its decisions should also be the work of the pope. These characteristics were not yet possible for the period of the early church, nor did they in fact apply. The eight ecumenical synods of the early church period were not convened, opened, guided and confirmed by the Roman pope but by the emperor (in individual cases more or less directly). The Byzantine emperors had an urgent interest in the disciplinary, cultic and dogmatic unity of the church, which is what the councils were mostly about, for reasons of political unity and stability, and regarded themselves as directly responsible for these matters (cf. Chapter III, 2). But not every council summoned by an emperor was an ecumenical council in the later sense. So the addition of individual councils to the list of ecumenical councils, i.e. their evaluation as universal synods representing the whole church, cannot be explained in terms of the way in which the synods understood or saw themselves or in terms of the spectrum of those who took part in them; rather, it derives from the way in which they were received, in other words the way in which the church subsequently came to regard them. The first four ecumenical councils, which will be discussed here, attained this status because of their central topics and because of their significant influence on later church history. Because of the content of their resolutions, in subsequent centuries they were even set above all other councils as a normative group. The decisions on the Christian faith formulated by them related to the Christian picture of God (the Trinity), christology, and with it the understanding of salvation (soteriology) and the Christian picture of the human being (theological anthropology). Pope Gregory the Great (590–604) compared these four councils with the four Gospels, Isidore of Seville (c. 560–636) with the four rivers in paradise. The view of the time was that the decisions of all later councils had to be measured by these four councils. This estimation is still undisputed in the Christian churches. It is true above all of the creed of the Council of Constantinople (381) that this is the only creed (or the last creed) to be shared by all Christians, so that it is the only common dogmatic basis for all churches. For individual Eastern churches only accept the consensus thus far, and reject Chalcedon with its creed (451).

However, this high esteem requires the ancient formulae and theology of the councils to be interpreted or translated into present-day language and made understandable to the modern mind. For they were formulated by men of late antiquity who thought in Greek, and whose world of questions, thought and language is not directly that of present-day Christians. The formulae of the ancient councils can be assimilated only through historical and theological explanations, through laborious reconstructions and intermediaries.

What was the process for finding the truth at the early church councils? There were no direct votes with numbers for and against.

First the opinions of the various parties were heard, and there was free discussion during which there were spontaneous expressions of approval and disapproval. Finally the majority emerged in the form of predominant acclamations. The position thus established by the majority of the council fathers was regarded by their party as an expression of the will of the Holy Spirit and as the indisputable truth of God which from then on was binding on all the churches.

2. *The first discussions on the question of the Trinity*

In the second half of the third century, controversial views were expressed in East and West about the Christian picture of God, in the form of the question of the relationship between Christ or the Logos and God (the Father). The New Testament and later tradition spoke of God (the Father), the Son (the Logos) and the Spirit, but the relationship between them was undefined and never clarified. In brief, hitherto this relationship had been seen as one between a Son who was also 'God' (or divine) and a Father to whom he was subordinate. This relationship of subordination was expressed in different ways, but the question had not been clarified in principle: there was evidently no need for this. The subordinationist view was first of all the whole church's way of believing in the Father and the Son (as yet no similar statements were made about the Spirit). It arose consistently out of the biblical-Jewish monotheism of Christians. Faith in the one God was taken for granted. Talk of the divine Logos and Spirit was compatible with monotheism in the model of subordination to the one God.

However, new questions arose in the third century. At that time various attempts were being made to understand the biblical statements and belief hitherto more accurately on this point. In a confused scene of controversies, very different dogmatic positions were put forward. The reason for this was the difference between the traditions of the particular churches, which varied widely in the conceptualities, thought-patterns and accents of their theology. There had not as yet been any unification through a doctrinal decision by the whole church. From the end of the second century, a theology was pointedly advocated which is called Monarchianism. This was concerned to maintain the unity, uniqueness and 'sole rule' (*monarchia*) of God in a way which corresponded to the biblical concept of God. It was partly a reaction to the Logos theology of the Apologists of the second century (see Chapter VII), who spoke of the Logos as a 'second God' alongside God (the Father). Many people felt that also to use the word 'God' for the Logos made the monarchy and uniqueness of God dangerously unclear. They sought to safeguard the uniqueness of God against this in two different ways. Either they disputed that Christ is personally God; divine forces were said to be at work in Jesus (dynamism) or he was said to have been later associated with God through adoption (adoptionism). In that case he was sufficiently far removed from God for God's 'monarchy' to remain unassailed. Or Christ was understood as one of the forms (*modus*) of God's appearance. The one God first revealed himself as Father, then as Son and finally as Spirit ('Modalism'), but is always one and the same. Monarchianism in one version or another was the theology widespread at the end of the second century and *de facto* also the general belief in the church communities. Those theologians who thus began to distinguish the Logos as God clearly from the Father or even to speak of a threeness (trinity) in God (as did Tertullian, Hippolytus and Novatian) thus came up against bitter resistance from the many simple believers, who charged them with teaching two or three gods (cf. Tertullian, *Adversus Praxean* 3.1; Hippolytus, *Refutatio* IX 11,3: 12.16). The beginnings of the church's theology of the Trinity were felt to be polytheism, and rejected as heresy in the name of the biblical God.

Modalism was also put forward by a Libyan called Sabellius, so this theology is also called Sabellianism after him. He came to Rome about 217 and was evidently the cause of the first controversies there, because his extreme Monarchianism was felt to be a deviation from the faith of the Roman community, in other words heresy. He was excommunicated by Callistus in Rome. Decades later (257) the dispute over his theology lived on in his homeland of Libya. The trinitarian question (the relationship between God, Son and Spirit) was posed more and more acutely. For example, some Sabellian Libyan bishops no longer ventured to speak of the 'Son of God' (as an independent figure). They and their opponents wrote a letter to Bishop Dionysius of Alexandria (who died in 264) for clarification. In his answers the bishop emphasized the real difference between

Father and Son (against Modalism). The Sabellians countered with the charge that Dionysius separated the Son from the Father, did not call him eternal, saw him as being different in nature from the Father, and claimed that the Son was not 'one in substance' (Greek *homoousios*) with the Father (which Dionysius denied). Here for the first time we find this important Greek term *homoousios* ('of the same substance'), which was to play a central role at Nicaea. The Libyan Sabellians sought confirmation from Bishop Dionysius of Rome (259–268), probably because they knew of Monarchian tendencies in Rome. Dionysius of Rome rejected both Sabellianism and the formulae of Dionysius of Alexandria as presented to him. He himself advocated a Monarchianism according to which the Logos had always belonged to the Father and might not be distanced from him. By contrast, Dionysius of Alexandria believed that the Logos was produced by the Father, was subordinate to the Father (Subordinationism), and remains different from him. After a correspondence the two came to an agreement, condemned Monarchianism and Subordinationism in extreme forms, which they regarded as illegitimate, but kept to their different theologies.

We can see here how close agreement and excommunication over these difficult positions were when dogmatic terminology had not been qualified. Dionysius of Alexandria was afraid that the term 'of the same substance' was being used in a Sabellian (= Modalistic way), but accepted it. He wanted to see the real trinity safeguarded in God and thus said that the unity of God is extended into trinity without being divided, and remains a unity without the trinity being confused. Dionysius of Rome also asserted trinity and unity in God. So both could come closer through their dispute, even if they could not find precise concepts. However, for the Sabellian bishops, talk of trinity already meant an intolerable division and multiplication in God, and they had the impression that this was talk of three Gods.

At the same time there was a conflict in Antioch (in Syria) over the same point. There Bishop Paul of Samosata (on the Euphrates; he died in 272) advocated a dynamistic Monarchianism, and the theologian Lucian, who is regarded as the founder of the 'Antiochene school' (see Chapter VII), advocated a Subordinationism. The conjunction and controversy between them was typical of the time. Now the question of the Trinity was being raised everywhere:

the problem existed; solutions differed; and theological vocabulary was unclear and not uniform. Paul of Samosata, who was condemned by the church in Antioch in 268, used the term *homoousios* for his dynamism. As a result, when this term arose later in connection with the Council of Nicaea it proved to be a loaded one. The central dogmatic problem of the fourth century, the question of unity and trinity in God, thus had its prehistory in the second and third centuries.

3. Arianism and the council in Nicaea (325)

This discussion over the question of God continued in new conditions in the fourth century, now as the so-called Arian dispute. This name stems from the fact that the new controversies and conflicts were sparked off by a presbyter named Arius in Alexandria. From about 318 he preached a clearly subordinationist theology, which I shall describe shortly, in his church district in the city of Alexandria. He immediately clashed with his bishop Alexander over it, and did not accept the dogmatic corrections required of him.

As the speedy and marked reaction of the whole church to this conflict shows, Arius was by no means alone in his theology; many people thought as he did. The use of the name 'Arianism' for the movement which now began is relatively coincidental, since Arius was just one of the most prominent advocates of the theology concerned. There was still no official orthodox church teaching on the question of the Trinity which was accepted everywhere; there were only rival traditions and schemes. Generally binding decisions were made only during the course of the conflict, which was sparked off politically by Arius. Thus Arius, who adopted a pointed dogmatic position, cannot be regarded from the start as a deviant from an established orthodoxy which already existed and had to be observed. He was a pupil of Lucian of Antioch, and convinced that in his Subordinationism he was advocating a venerable old theology. At the same time he was certain that he was taking up Alexandrian tradition, since he knew that an earlier predecessor of his bishop, Dionysius of Alexandria, had also advocated Subordinatianism (though we must qualify this by saying 'at first'). So Arius could believe that he was in the right. However, his bishop Alexander could refer to the same Dionysius of Alexandria for a contrary theology, since he had assented to the *homoousios*, a formula which excluded Subordinationism. We can see simply from the Alexandrian tradition how difficult it could be in specific instances to decide between orthodoxy and heresy.

So Arius took up a particular tradition of dogmatic thought which existed alongside others. And the provocation caused by his theology in the meantime to the advocates of another doctrine of the Trinity led to dogmatic and church-political controversies of an unprecedented dimension, with devastating consequences for the unity and peace of Christians. In addition there were the political implications that for reasons connected with the imperial ideology and for political opportunism, the emperor Constantine was interested in settling the conflict. As we saw, Constantine first trivialized it and then resolutely took its resolution in hand by summoning the Council of Nicaea and clearly guiding its course.

The theology of Arius was concerned with the ontological subordination of the Son in favour of God (the Father). To this end Arius formulated a series of exclusive properties or characteristics of God: the Father alone is unbegotten, uncreated, eternal, without a beginning; that means that he is 'alone true God', for 'he is absolutely the only one, the origin (*arche*)', namely the origin of all that is. Now the Son is not all that, but he is created and has come into being. One provocative formulation of Arius was: 'He (the Son) was not before he was begotten', and another 'There was a time when he was not.' Along with many others, Arius saw this statement supported by Proverbs 8.22: 'The Lord created me as the beginning of his ways.' With this scriptural proof and with other statements Arius sought to distinguish the Son from all other created beings and make him superior to them; but his subordination to God was just as as important and correct. The Son is certainly the most perfect creature, but he is also qualitatively different from the other creatures, though he is a creature and came into being. So Arianism is Subordinationism.

It can be claimed that the thought of Arius was philosophical and very academic, since his assertions result from a way of thinking which 'construed' the world from the supreme being, from transcendence, in the style of the philosophy of the time. Here the supreme being (God) remained singular and was not attained by any other being. Especially since the second century, Christians had followed John 1.1,14 in calling the Son Logos and seeking to mediate between Christianity and philosophy through this term. For philosophy (in a variety of views) spoke of intermediary beings between transcendence and the world which could similarly be termed Logos and which ontologically occupied an intermediate position between 'God' and the world. However, for biblical Christian creation faith this ontological middle position did not exist; such faith knew only the alternatives of God and creation, and any third element was excluded. Against this background Christian theology had to decide whether the Logos of the Bible stands on the side of God or on that of creatures. Arius believed that the Logos stood on the side of creation; his opponents and the council in Nicaea believed that the Logos stood on the side of God. Bishop Alexander and the other anti-Arians thought more in pastoral (and less in philosophical) terms in the sense that they argued from the significance of the Son for salvation to his deity: if the Son is not truly God, then the redemption of humankind is an illusion, because only God can save it from its disastrous situation.

A synod of about 100 Egyptian and Libyan bishops under Alexander of Alexandria condemned Arius as a heretic. The whole, initially small, group of his local followers was excommunicated: two bishops, five priests and six deacons. Arius did not accept the condemnation and attempted to win over like-minded theologians elsewhere. These existed, like the Origenist Eusebius of Caesarea in Palestine and above all Eusebius of Nicomedia, a skilful and decisive politician. There were synods in various places which rehabilitated Arius in protest against the judgment in Alexandria. As a result of this, and through the counter-reactions to these Arian measures, the confusion again increased. Propaganda and partisan support were passionate.

So to put an end to the dispute, for the first time Constantine arranged a synod of the whole church of the empire which through its ceremonial he stylized as a vision of the future: he demonstrated to the empire the peaceful, happy unity of emperor and bishops as pillars of the realm and its support. However, the council was not as comprehensive and representative as all that. It was opened on 20

May 325 with around 300 bishops, approximately a third of whom came from the immediate vicinity (Asia Minor). The rest came from other Eastern churches; at most only five bishops came from the Latin West (they probably just happened to be staying at the imperial court). For reasons which we do not know, Pope Silvester I (314–335) had himself represented, as did the popes at subsequent councils of the early church.

All the theological trends which were concerned with the doctrine of the Trinity at the time were represented at Nicaea. Neither the supporters nor the opponents of Arius were homogeneous groups. The opponents included Bishop Alexander of Alexandria (with his deacon Athanasius, whom he brought along to the council) and Ossius of Cordoba, both of whom had immediately presented Arianism as a dramatic danger for the church and had adopted counter-measures. They were supported by the representatives of a resolute and sometimes even fanatical Monarchianism (Sabellianism, Modalism) who theologically were even further removed from the Arian distinction of the Son (as creature) from the Father because they did not really distinguish between the Father and the Son (in Modalistic fashion); in some respects they included Eustathius of Antioch and above all Marcellus of Ancyra (condemned for Sabellianism in 336). All in all, the non-Arians or anti-Arians were in the majority.

It is essential to note in the course and result of the Council of Nicaea that after hard debates on the disputed question the council fathers took as their basis an already existing creed (*symbolum*, which was perhaps that of the church of Eusebius of Caesarea in Palestine). They supplemented this creed with some statements or formulae which made it more clearly and sharply anti-Arian. The text already said of the Son that he was 'God of God' and (metaphorically) 'light of light'. This intrinsically clear formulation was not emphatic enough for the fathers in the situation of the dispute. They therefore supplemented it, though we cannot determine with certainty the precise extent of their additions. At all events the formula now became

True God of true God,
begotten, not made,
being of one substance (*homoousios*) with the Father.

In these lines from the Nicene creed we have the theology of the council. It was formulated against the Arians or Eusebians. Here the term *homoousios* is decisive and the context makes it unequivocal. The Son is of one substance with the Father, God like God the Father, and is really distinct from him as a separate 'person', though this term was used only later. This theology corresponded precisely to notions in the Western church, in which since Tertullian the attribute *consubstantialis* (of the same being) or *eiusdem substantiae* had been used of the Son.

The emperor Constantine had taken part in the course of the council and in its result. There is some evidence that he helped to establish the term *homoousios*. At the end he supported the result with his imperial authority. As a clear demonstration he banished Arius and the two bishops from among his immediate followers who were the only ones not to have subscribed to the creed of Nicaea. The church-political and dogmatic problem seemed to have been settled with the peaceful outcome of the council. The emperor celebrated the twentieth anniversary of his reign with the bishops before they went home. But the harmony was deceptive.

4. *The crisis after Nicaea and discussion about the Spirit*

The consensus which had apparently been reached and which had proved decisive as a result of Constantine's presence was a fragile one. Only three months after the council, Eusebius of Nicomedia and two other bishops withdrew their signatures, which they had never been able to offer with conviction; they were banished that same year. There was strong opposition to Nicaea, and wearisome periods of crisis began for the church.

First of all the Arians and groups with a similar position could not assent to the council for dogmatic reasons, and rejected the term *homoousios*. However, the 'conservatives' also had serious objections in principle to the fact that this word represented the use in a creed of a philosophical term which did not occur in the Bible. This objection made it difficult or impossible for many people to accept the Council of Nicaea, though they agreed with the substance of what was said there. The term was further discredited in that Paul of Samosata had used it in a heretical sense (see VIII, 2 above) and its occurrence in

Gnostic doctrinal systems made its use in the church's confession seem suspicious. The council as a whole was rejected along with the term. Furthermore, the Nicene party did not do very much to defend and clarify the creed and thus to commend this term in particular. Whereas the whole of the Latin West along with Egypt maintained Nicaea with a striking certainty and found no problems with it, having with a sure sense answered the relevant questions along the lines of the council at a relatively early stage, the hard debates over the Trinity (as later also those over christology, see 6 and 7 below) with their enormous speculative complications were carried on in the churches of the East. They arose from Greek questions and were carried on along the lines of a type of thought which was interested in Greek philosophy. (By its nature, Latin Christianity was much more concerned with problems of church practice, the concept of the church, morality and sin, holiness and redemption, grace and freedom.)

Opposition to the council could chalk up its successes. A mere three years after Nicaea, the emperor Constantine resolved to adopt a pro-Arian policy, even though he had not only assented to the theology of the council but had also been the key factor in influencing it, though without really knowing anything about dogma. We may suppose that the reasons for his change of course in religious policy at the expense of the Nicenes were as follows. In the meantime he may have come more strongly under the influence of Arians (Eusebius of Nicomedia) than of Nicenes; pehaps he also recognized that the theology of Arius with its hierarchical sub-ordinationist construction better matched his own political ideology, according to which the monarchical emperor represents the monarchy of God on earth (one God, one emperor, one empire); the pragmatic consideration that the Arians were clearly in the majority in the East may also have proved a decisive factor, so that the emperor came to the conclusion that he could bring about unity in the empire only with them, not against them. Arius, Eusebius of Nicomedia and their banished followers were rehabilitated by the emperor after subscribing to very vague formulae of faith. Over very wide areas all the Nicene bishops were deposed. One of those concerned, who was a prominent opponent of this anti-Nicene policy, was Athanasius (295–373), from 328 Bishop of Alexandria.

Under Constantine and his successors he went into exile five times, for seventeen years in all. At ever new councils the bishops sought formulae and definitions, but above all constantly went through a process in which very often it was not so much that actual dogmatic differences were discussed but rather personal accusations and slanders of a moral and political kind were made. This was a style of church polemics and power politics which had meanwhile become widespread. From Constantine on, the emperors took part by supporting or weakening parties through the deposition and appointment of bishops.

Constantine died in 337. He was succeeded by two of his sons. In the West the emperor Constans (337–350) was a resolute Nicene and thus at one with the church there. But in the East Constantius II (337–361) emphatically strengthened Arianism. Under him for the first time the church (i.e. the Nicene church) massively felt the powerful pressure of a Christian emperor on anything that did not correspond to his policy and that he regarded as heresy (see III, 2, d). After becoming sole ruler in 350, Constantius also exercised this pressure on the Western, Nicene, church by compelling bishops at synods to subscribe to Arian formulae and condemnations of Athanasius. Refusal was punished with banishment or imprisonment. Liberius of Rome (352–366) was one of the main victims. There were some uncompromising and resolute opponents in the West like Lucifer of Cagliari, Hilary of Poitiers and Ossius of Cordoba. They all had to suffer severely as 'martyrs' of their orthodoxy. Thus the emperor attempted with brutal means to make Arianism the one creed of the empire.

Arius had died as early as 335, Eusebius of Caesarea around 339 and Eusebius of Nicomedia at the end of 341. But the discussion, the introduction of constantly new formulae and the exchange of hostilities at the councils continued. The Western church consistently held to Nicaea, but in the East there were increasing attempts to create a new formula in opposition to the council. The proposals for this were not crudely Arian nor openly anti-Nicene; they tended more to follow a conservative line. In other words, they refrained from being as precise as traditional formulae were in defining the relationship between Father and Son. But that was no longer possible, because the state of the question had moved on.

This tiny extract from the proceedings and party ploys can indicate how deep the crisis over Arianism was even after Nicaea. Another reason why the situation remained so fluid and confused was fundamentally the lack of decisiveness in imperial religious policy, without which no trend could establish itself definitively. The discussion over the relationship between the Father and the Son also entailed the raising of a similar question about the Holy Spirit. What was the relationship of the Spirit to the Father and the Son? Around 360 this topic seems to have been a further complication in the debate, first in Egypt and rather later in Asia Minor. There were those who defended the identity of substance (*homoousia*) of the Spirit with the Father (and the Son) and those who opposed it. The former called the latter Pneumatomachoi = 'those who dispute (the consubstantiality) of the Spirit'. Basil of Caesarea (c.330–379) was foremost in developing the consubstantiality or divinity of the Spirit both theoretically and on a biblical basis, and thus played a normative part in preparations for the Second Ecumenical Council. Along with other bishops he steadfastly advocated the Nicene tendency in the East. This tendency was unexpectedly and decisively supported by a change of emperor. With Theodosius the Great (emperor 379–395), a Spaniard, i.e. a member of the Western church and thus a convinced Nicene, became the new emperor of the East, and in an edict of 28 February 380 he obliged all inhabitants of the empire to accept the Nicene creed, thus creating the state church. In his edict *Cunctos populos* this emperor already described the Nicene faith as belief in 'the one Godhead (*unam deitatem*) of the Father, the Son and the Holy Spirit in equal majesty and holy Trinity (*sub parili maiestate et sub pia trinitate*)'. This represented a crude change of course at the expense of the Arians, accompanied by the expulsion of their bishops and the other disadvantages under which the Nicenes had previously had to suffer. The convening of the Council of Constantinople was a clear sign of the new policy.

5. *The council in Constantinople (381)*

Theodosius convened a council in Constantinople in 381 to put an end to the dispute over Arianism and normalize conditions in the church. Of the aims which he set this council, here we need discuss only the restoration of the unity of the faith. Unity was to be attained by the condemnation and exclusion of all trends with subordinationist Arian tendencies.

No acts or documents have survived from this council, in particular the text adopted at it over the *homoousia* (consubstantiality) of Father, Son and Spirit. The council united over the wording of an already existing creed which was composed after 362. This creed was quoted seventy years later at the Fourth Ecumenical Council in Chalcedon and included in its records as the faith of 'the holy fathers of Constantinople' (see below, VIII, 7) and thus has been remembered as the creed of the Second Ecumenical Council. But the council did not compose this formula, adopting, rather, an existing text. And it was only through its reception at Chalcedon that the Council of Constantinople was given a special status and promoted to being an ecumenical council. Taken by itself it was a partisan synod, and moreover was attended only by Eastern bishops. Church reception plays a normative role in the assessment of a synod as an ecumenical synod (see above VIII, 1).

The creed referred to is the 'great' or Niceno-Constantinopolitan creed. It is still used in the liturgy and is the only really ecumenical creed, i.e. the only one accepted by all Christian churches. It contains the formula of Nicaea almost word for word, but notably extends it in an anti-Arian direction. The new dogmatic element (after the dispute against the Pneumatomachoi) consists in the statements about the *homoousia* of the Spirit. Whereas nothing was said about this at Nicaea, which had only said 'We believe . . . in the Holy Spirit', the formulation is now extensive and precise:

> We believe . . . in the Holy Spirit
> the Lord,
> the Giver of Life,
> proceeding from the Father,
> who with the Father and the Son is worshipped and glorified,
> who spoke by the prophets.

Individually and together these statements contain a statement of the divinity of the Spirit. With this council the dogma of the Trinity was formed.

6. The christological question

Both chronologically and in content the trinitarian debate which was resolved in Nicaea and Constantinople overlapped with the christological discussion about the appropriate dogmatic expression of the special character and significance of Jesus Christ. This question, too, was raised at that time against the background of the Greek thought of late antiquity, namely as a question about his *nature*. The biblical statements about Jesus of Nazareth, about his life and work, his faith and his mission, his origin from God and his resurrection, were interpreted as statements about his special *being*. His significance for salvation was seen as lying in the singular character of his nature. In particular it was asked how it was possible to express the unity of Christ in view of the two realities – divine and human – in him or how there could be two realities uncurtailed in one and the same Christ. The statements about the Trinity had already helped to determine normatively the substance, the nature of Christ: Christ is God as the Father is God. Then the christological question in the narrower sense arose because certain questions remained open after the completion of the dogma of the Trinity.

The christological question had already been posed in the schemes of the second and third centuries and then again by Arianism, which in its notion of the Trinity understood Christ as a creature, not as God. There were a large number of christological doctrines and heresies causing a chain reaction of assessment and repudiation. But the christological question became really acute in the fourth century, remarkably because of a Nicene, Apollinaris of Laodicea (who died around 390). With Nicaea, Apollinaris maintained Christ's *homoousia* with the Father, i.e. his divinity. For the sake of this divinity he now put forward the view that in the incarnation the Logos did not assume a ('whole') man but an incomplete human nature. The human nature assumed lacked a human soul. In Jesus Christ the Logos performed the functions performed by the soul in the body. Apollinaris believed that this was the only way of keeping the human nature assumed by the Logos from the split into good and evil from which all human beings suffer and which vitiates them. If the Logos himself is dominant and directly governs and guides the human nature,

Apollinarius

then Jesus Christ is not affected by the sinful weakness of human nature.

These ideas were received sympathetically and were developed both moderately and more radically. But from 362 on the Nicenes, among whom Apollinaris belonged over the question of the Trinity, refuted him with an argument which was then continually advanced against Apollinarianism and related christology: only that which has been assumed by the Logos (Christ) can be redeemed by him. So if he has assumed only a torso of human nature (without a soul), then the human being as a whole is not saved. The criterion of certainty of salvation played a key role in the christology of the early church. Apollinarianism was condemned on many occasions at synods (in 377 in Rome, 378 in Alexandria, 379 in Antioch, in 381 at the Second Ecumenical Synod in Constantinople), and was suppressed legally by Emperor Theodosius I. The Apollinarians continued as a sect until 420.

Diodore of Tarsus (who died before 394) emphasized against Arianism the divinity of Christ and against Apollinaris the integrity of a complete human nature which the Logos had assumed. This marked and emphatic distinction between divinity and humanity in Christ was from now on a typical characteristic of the Antiochene 'school' or tradition (see Chapter VII) to which Diodore belonged. The Antiochenes maintained the clear distinction by stating that Jesus Christ is the Son of God and son of a human mother. In this way they wanted to confess both divinity and humanity at the same time, but without describing any division in Christ. However, contemporaries, particularly in Alexandria, suspected or accused them of 'splitting' and 'dividing' Christ. Diodore certainly asserted that 'there are not two Sons', but the Antiochene christology remained vulnerable because it had not succeeded in formulating the unity in Christ while at the same time maintaining the distinction. From now on the christological problem remained that of clarifying the duality and the unity in Christ. Here it was typical that the Antiochenes were concerned to distinguish the divine and the human, while the Alexandrians safeguarded the unity at the expense of the duality (at any rate, that is what the Antiochenes thought).

The Antiochene line on christology continued through Theodore of Mopsuestia (who died in 428). He made a clear distinction in the incarnate Logos between the divine and the human nature, and against Arians and Apollinarians put all the emphasis on the fact that the Logos had assumed a complete human nature; at the same time he intended to express the unity of the two natures, but he emphasized it with the word 'union' (Greek *synapheia*), which in the eyes of his opponents was much too weak and inaccurate. Those who held other opinions constantly argued that Antiochene christology intended and led to a division in Christ. A nervous, polemical climate of polarization prevailed, in which those on one side virtually waited for dogmatic or political 'mistakes' on the part of their opponents. Theodore was posthumously condemned at the Fifth Ecumenical Council in 553.

The Alexandrians saw a weak point of the Antiochenes becoming open heresy when Theodore's pupil Nestorius (who died after 451) occupied the see of Constantinople (428). The occupancy of this see was always a political matter of the first order, not least because Alexandria and Constantinople were constant rivals for pre-eminence. Immediately after becoming bishop Nestorius had to decide whether the title Mother of God (Greek *theotokos*) could be used for Mary. As an Antiochene he had reservations, not so much about its dogmatic legitimacy, but because it was open to misunderstanding. He felt that it was misleading, because one could say only of the humanity in Christ and not of the divinity that Christ was born of Mary. He was also afraid that the title would lead to mythical notions about a mother of gods. Therefore by way of mediation he proposed the title 'Mother of Christ' (*christotokos*), because the name Christ denoted the two natures in union. The Alexandrians protested dramatically against this: they saw it as a blatant denial of the unity of Christ and a division of Christ. There were also objections from the side of popular piety, which loved the old title 'Mother of God' for Mary. This dispute, the details of which we need not investigate here, sparked off the christological controversies which led to council decisions.

It is important to have the following background to the theological side of the debate. Because the Antiochenes distinguished the natures in Christ so sharply, they had their reservations about a usage of christological language which was taken for granted elsewhere (above all in Alexandria), known as the *communicatio idiomatum*. According to this practice, because of the close union in Jesus Christ, the properties of his two natures could be expressed reciprocally. Under a name of Christ denoting only one of his two natures, the properties of the other nature could also be expressed. So it could be said that 'the Logos of God has been crucified'; 'the Logos has suffered'. In these two cases, statements about Christ's human nature are made under a name of Christ (the Logos of God) which refers to the divine nature. The coming councils would confirm this possibility, and it is still part of the dogmatic language of the church. On this presupposition the title 'Mother of God' (God has been born of Mary) was not only admissible but (from the Alexandrian perspective) virtually a test case of how seriously the Antiochenes took the unity in Christ. And the Alexandrians saw Nestorius's objections to the title as a denial of this unity of natures. He was 'dividing Christ', and thereupon was branded an arch-heretic. Modern scholarship has subsequently been able to show that Nestorius did not advocate the heresy imputed to him, i.e. the division or splitting of Christ into two natures. He was orthodox – even according to the criteria of his own time. Others certainly put forward a Nestorian christology, but Nestorius was no 'Nestorian'.

Protest and indignation over Nestorius was expressed especially by the then Patriarch of Alexandria, Cyril. Rome also expressed its view, in favour of Cyril; Nestorius had failed to inform Rome as accurately about his standpoint as Cyril had informed Rome about his own. One can call Cyril's (Alexandrian) christology, which was also advocated elsewhere, even in Constantinople, a theocentric one. The starting point of all statements is the divinity of the Logos. This was in accord with old tradition, since even subordinationist christologies (as in the case of the Apologists in the second century or Origen in the third) called the Logos divine or God. It makes the strength of Cyril's position understandable. However, the Antiochenes discovered a weakness of great danger here: if the divinity dominates in christology to such a degree, and if it is hardly possible to talk about the humanity of Christ, or at any rate to do so consistently, then the picture of Christ made man becomes incomplete and mutilated. The Antiochenes warned that to preserve orthodoxy, the humanity in Christ must not be allowed to be swallowed up in the Godhead.

The two options, Antiochene and Alexandrian, were not intrinsically contradictory: the reasons why those who advocated them felt that they had to be mutually exclusive were not primarily theological. It can perhaps be said that Antiochene christology was concerned to keep close to the Bible (the 'historical Jesus' of the Gospels) and to take the entrance of God into human history seriously. Alexandrian christology came from a spirituality of the ascent of human beings through Christ so that they become like God ('divinization'), and here understandably theology was essentially more concerned with the divinity of Jesus Christ than with his manhood.

Cyril reacted to Nestorius rapidly and energetically. He found a response and a following with the help of letters and dogmatic statements which he sent to opponents and potential supporters (especially among the Egyptian monks, in Rome and at the imperial court). A first success was that on 11 August 430 a Roman synod condemned Nestorius and called on him to repudiate his teaching, threatening to deposed him from his see. Cyril consolidated his public dogmatic argument, and among other things resorted to the traditional formulation 'One is the nature of the divine Logos made flesh'. The Antiochenes could not find the duality of God and man in his theology. For them Cyril's theses contained much that was unclear and suspicious. So Nestorius did not recant. The Antiochenes (including Theodoret of Cyrrhus, who died around 466) did not feel that they had been refuted by Cyril and thought that they had to fight against the heresy that they recognized in Alexandrian christology, and Cyril attacked them in return. Agitation continued with letters, diplomatic means and intrigues. Disunion and hostility were widespread. On the basis of former models it occurred to the emperor that he should summon a universal synod in order to restore the unity in which he was interested.

7. The councils in Ephesus (431) and Chalcedon (451)

On 19 November 430 Emperor Theodosius II convened a council at Ephesus for the following year. Events leading up to it were turbulent, as was its course. In the rivalry between the church parties, Cyril was the better tactician and somewhat less scrupulous in the use of power and even force than his opponents. He created a decisive advantage for himself in Ephesus before the beginning of the council. The bishops from Syria and the surrounding region who had combined forces as supporters of Nestorius under Bishop John of Antioch did not hasten on their journey because they expected nothing good of the council. Nor were the delegates from Rome there. Cyril took advantage of this, and opened the council on his own initiative on 22 June 431, before the Eastern (i.e. Syrian and Palestinian) and Roman representatives had arrived. The council should have examined the justification of Cyril's accusations against Nestorius. With his coup, Cyril had reversed the roles; Nestorius was to be examined and had to justify himself.

The Eastern bishops arrived five days later and the Romans two days after that. Cyril's synod condemned Nestorius, who refused to appear there, and deposed him. The Roman representatives endorsed this judgment because it corresponded with that of the Roman synod of 430 (see above VIII, 6). For their part, the Eastern bishops opened a synod of their own in Ephesus at which they deposed Cyril and the local bishop Memnon of Ephesus. Cyril's synod reacted by deposing John of Antioch and his supporters. The confusion was great, and was to become even more grotesque. When both sides appealed to the emperor, he had Nestorius, Cyril and Memnon imprisoned. This did not help negotiations. The populace and monks took part in the proceedings because their faith was affected by the theological questions. Finally the emperor joined the majority Alexandrian party, but did not condemn the Eastern bishops. Since union and reconciliation were impossible, bitterly disappointed, he dismissed the bishops with a sharp rebuke and closed the council in October 431. In the end Cyril's party had won, since the emperor still kept Nestorius in prison and replaced him in Constantinople with a bishop acceptable to the Alexandrians. Nestorius died in exile in Egypt, at the earliest in 451.

It is rather difficult to evaluate these events of the Third Ecumenical Council. In fact two parallel councils were being held. Both were strictly partisan, not ecumenical. But Cyril's council has been counted the ecumenical one (on the basis of its subsequent dogmatic confirmation and reception). What is its significance? The only result was the condemnation of Nestorius and the confirmation of the title 'Mother of God', but no text or creed was formulated. There were theologically more important councils of the early period. However, it attained this high rank through its subsequent reputation in the early church. Moreover it had a subsequent history which is part of it, and sheds some light on the way in which it has been evaluated. The new pope (Sixtus III, 432–440) and the emperor again took up the concern for peace and union. There were laborious new negotiations between Cyril and John of Antioch – one of the rare examples of a concern for unity instead of confrontation at this time. Both sides made concessions: the Antiochenes did not object to the condemnation of Nestorius, and Cyril refrained from insisting on certain statements. It is worth noting that Cyril gave his assent to a creed from Antioch. In 433 there was an important Formula of Union. It was, one might say, a belated result of Ephesus in 431. Theologically it marks a decisive step forward; both the distinction between Godhead and manhood in Christ and also the unity in him are equally emphasized. This was not a compromise, but an attempt at a synthesis of the disputed perspectives. The central statements of this Formula of Union run:

> We confess . . . our Lord Jesus Christ
> – as perfect God and perfect man
> – consubstantial (*homoousios*) with the Father . . . as to his Godhead and consubstantial with us as to his manhood:
> – there is a unity of the two natures,
> – therefore we confess one Christ, one Son, one Lord
> – on the basis of this unconfused unity we confess the holy virgin as Mother of God.

These statements combined both positions and also satisfactorily met the fears of each about the other. But there were extremists on both sides who protested against the formula. The union could not be implemented in church-political terms and thus was relatively ineffective. Nor was its diction really clear against the background of the ongoing controversies. At all events, for the time being the debate went on.

The next phase was played out with new names: the pope in Rome was now Leo the Great (440–461); John of Antioch died in 441/2 and Cyril (who died in 444) was followed as bishop of Alexandria by Dioscurus, whose political actions were even harsher than those of Cyril; in Constantinople Flavian became bishop in 446. The dispute broke out afresh when in 447/48 an old monk Eutyches advanced a provocative christology in Constantinople. He was a resolute anti-Nestorian, a supporter of Cyril and an extreme opponent of the Formula of Union of 433. He advocated his position in such an uncompromising way that one has to regard it as Monophysitism: humanity and divinity in Christ together form only one nature (which in fact meant that only the divine nature was recognized: in Christ there is one nature, the divine one). How markedly the human nature of Christ was reduced in this christology is evident from an image used by the Monophysites: in Christ the humanity is taken up into the divinity, as a drop of sweet water is dissolved in the salty ocean. Eutyches presented it in the version that Christ is 'from two natures', meaning that before the union, before the incarnation, there were two natures, which combined in Christ into a single nature; in the union only the divine nature remains. In Eutyches Alexandrian theology fell victim to its perpetual temptation: explicit Monophysitism.

A synod in Constantinople condemned Eutyches on 22 November 448; however, he was given massive protection by Dioscurus, who in fact advocated precisely the same theology. Eutyches got the emperor Theodosius to summon an ecumenical council at Ephesus in 449. Pope Leo the Great did not just send a delegation to the council, as his predecessors has done, but composed a dogmatic treatise on the christological problem which included his own position and sent it to Bishop Flavian of Constantinople. It has become famous as the Tome of Leo or the Dogmatic Epistle to Flavian. This work demonstrates Leo's excellent knowledge of the problem: it is conceptually clear and, as history showed, took things further. The council which had been summoned was so packed with Eutyches' supporters that it was certain that the extremely partisan Dioscurus would be president and that representatives of other trends would be excluded. For example the old Antiochene Theodoret of Cyrrhus was prohibited from taking part. The way Dioscurus guided the discussion was of a piece with this. The bishops of the council were no Monophysites, but Dioscurus intimidated them, stifled any resistance and prevented several attempts by the Roman representatives to read the Tome of Leo, which dogmatically did not suit him. Under this regime the council rehabilitated Eutyches, deposed all the important Antiochenes (like Flavian and Theodoret) and branded them as Nestorians. There was a storm of protest, since many parties were affected: the Antiochenes, the Roman pope, the episcopate of Gaul and Italy, and Valentinian III, the emperor of the West. But Theodosius II, the emperor of the East, stood by the council of 449. It went down in history as the Robber Synod. For the non-Monophysites the situation seemed hopeless.

Then in 450 Theodosius II died. The political change of power very soon made everything look different. Under the empress Pulcheria and the emperor Marcian some lost influence and others gained it. The imperial court made contact with the pope in Rome. A new course was set in church politics, aimed at a new council and supported by the majority of bishops. The imperial couple convened the council, the Fourth Ecumenical Council, which met from 8 October to 1 November 451 in Chalcedon near Constantinople. With more than 500 bishops, predominantly from the Eastern churches, and under the leadership of imperial commissioners, the first part of it was devoted to banishing the Robber Synod of 449 to oblivion (it was therefore not recognized as an ecumenical synod, although it claimed to be). Flavian was rehabilitated and Dioscurus deposed.

More important was the quest for a creed on which all could agree. The Tome of Leo evidently played a significant constructive role in the negotiations, in a form which showed how it corresponded with Cyril. At Chalcedon, Cyril was invoked as the witness to orthodoxy and with him the 431 Council of Ephesus. After great difficulties a commission drafted a dogmatic text which then found recognition, albeit laboriously. This is the 451 Chalcedonian Definition of Faith. It begins with a preamble which is interesting above all because it cites the two creeds of Nicaea (325) and Constantinople (381) from the orthodox tradition. Then it describes the two errors of Nestorianism and Monophysitism in order to reject them; finally follows the formulation of faith proper. This formula first describes the unity and distinction in Christ and confirms the title 'Mother of God', very much in the style of the 433 Formula of Union, partly in verbal agreement with it:

> We all unanimously teach that . . . Jesus Christ . . .
> is perfect in Godhead and perfect in manhood,
> the selfsame truly God and truly man . . .
> consubstantial (*homoousios*) with the Father according to the Godhead
> and consubstantial (*homoousios*) with us according to the manhood;
> . . . before the ages begotten of the Father as to the Godhead,
> but in the last days . . .
> born of the Virgin Mary, Theotokos as to the manhood.

Then the Definition continues in original formulae which had not yet appeared in a church creed:

> Acknowledged in two natures
> unconfusedly, unchangeably, indivisibly, inseparably;
> the difference of the Natures being in no way removed because of the Union,
> but rather the property of each nature being preserved,
> and both concurring into one person (*prosopon*) and one hypostasis:
> not as though he were parted or divided into two persons,
> but one and the selfsame Son and Only-begotten God, Word, Lord, Jesus Christ.

It is easy to recognize where the text differs from Nestorianism and Monophysitism, as unity and duality in Christ are stressed: he is 'one person' 'in two natures'. The two decisive terms in the definition, person (*prosopon*) and nature (*physis*), have a philosophical quality. At its councils the early church enquired in Greek fashion into the significance of Jesus for salvation by ontologically asking about his particular being and nature. The answer matched the question: Christ is an individual with a singular structure of being.

On 25 October 451 this confession was solemnly proclaimed as the confession of the imperial council, with imperial ceremonial and invocations of the great hour of orthodoxy. But Chalcedon did not mean the end of christological disputes. The council of universal peace had not been achieved, either ecclesiastically or politically. The history of the period after Chalcedon is the history of a widespread refusal to recognize the council. The late fifth and sixth centuries were largely taken up with this crisis. The state did all it could to impose the council formula, but in vain. The strongest opposition came from Egypt, whose church stood solid against the condemnation of its patriarch Dioscurus and kept to its particular theology (with a Monophysite tendency). In terms of this historical opposition the Coptic church in Egypt is still a 'pre-Chalcedonian' church in its creed, following Cyril's christology of a 'unity' of natures. At the time there was also resistance to Chalcedon in Palestine and Syria. It was backed by theologians, but also had the sympathies of the monks and church people. Ascetic spiritual popular traditions had deeply rooted the idea of the divinization of human beings or their godlikeness and made the conciliar doctrine of two natures always look like an impairment of Christ and human salvation. Here total divinization was the key notion of all theology. Even imperial policy sometimes fluctuated between Chalcedon and Monophysitism. Concern for union and sympathies with Alexandrian-Monophysite tendencies gave rise to a movement which sought to provide a bridge by interpreting Chalcedon in a way which was thought to promise a universal consensus over the council. Because of the new interpretation this theology is called neo-Chalcedonian. Its perspectives and emphases were those of the dominant theology of sixth-century Eastern orthodoxy. The Chalcedonian Definition's formulation of the natures was too crude, too rough in its terminology for this approach. It took up Cyril's phrase of the 'one nature', with which it felt that Chalcedon had to be clarified.

Whereas the Monophysites regarded the Chalcedonian Definition as Nestorian, and missed the decisive accents of their great Cyril in the council, the neo-Chalcedonians regarded Cyril and the council as compatible. Above all they thought it right that some formulae or statements of Cyril's should be added to the Council of Chalcedon which Cyril himself had avoided for the sake of peace and the 433 Formula of Union. So here Cyril with his pointed demarcations from Nestorianism once again had his day. The characteristic of the neo-Chalcedonian movement, which was mainly supported by Egyptian monks, was a theology which did not attach any importance to making the distinction in Christ precise. It drew all the consequences of the *communicatio idiomatum*, and preferred statements like 'One of the Trinity (the Logos, i.e. God) has suffered' (its adherents were known as Theopaschites = advocates of the doctrine that God has suffered). The oneness in Christ was understood in such a way that dogmatically there was no concern for a distinction of the two natures.

Neo-Chalcedonianism did not achieve the desired union with the Monophysites, but contributed to the suppression of Nestorianism. The most important sixth-century church politician, who at the same time was one of the most notable theologians of neo-Chalcedonianism, was the emperor Justinian I (527–565), who vainly sought agreement with the Monophysites at the Fifth Ecumenical Council in Constantinople in 553. Throughout church history a division into Chalcedonian, Monophysite and Nestorian churches has remained; in conclusion, we should note that the historical reasons for the permanent division are not just the dogmatic ones discussed here, but political, national and emotional factors.

Bibliography

T. H. Bindley and F. W. Green (eds.), *Ecumenical Documents of the Faith*, Methuen 1950

Aloys Grillmeier, *Christ in Christian Tradition*, Volume 1, Mowbray and John Knox Press ²1975

J. N. D. Kelly, *Early Christian Doctrines*, A.& C. Black ⁵1977

R. A. Norris (ed.), *The Christological Controversy*, Fortress Press 1980

G. L. Prestige, *God in Patristic Thought*, SPCK 1936

William Rusch (ed.), *The Trinitarian Controversy*, Fortress Press 1980

Maurice Wiles, *The Making of Christian Doctrine*, Cambridge University Press 1967

Rowan Williams, *Arius: Heresy and Tradition*, Darton, Longman and Todd 1987

Frances Young, *From Nicaea to Chalcedon*, SCM Press and Fortress Press 1983
Frances Young, *The Making of the Creeds*, SCM Press and Trinity Press International 1991

Conclusion

By the sixth century, Christianity had become the religion of the ancient world and had spread far beyond its frontiers. In this period it shaped the decisive elements of its identity as a church: constitution, liturgy, confession (dogma), biblical canon, theological method and relationship to society and culture. This process gave rise to very lasting traditions and continuities, but in the discussion of controversial interpretations in this early period it also led Christianity to lose its unity, which it never regained.

From the end of the fourth century, changed political conditions emerged. As a result of the migrations in the West, i.e. in Gaul, Spain, Africa and Italy, Germanic kingdoms came into being against which the Roman empire could not stand. After the loss of the old Roman political cohesion of these countries, the church was the only focus of unity and identity for the indigenous population. The new invaders were partly Christianized, but because of their Arian confession were no nearer to the citizens of the empire than the barbarians. In this twofold foreign rule, which was both political and religious, the function of the church in providing unity was extremely important socially.

At the same time the Eastern half of the empire remained relatively intact. The Eastern church continued to exist under a Roman emperor in an empire with the old frontiers. There, along with the Graeco-Roman tradition, it was the foundation for early Byzantine history and culture. So political conditions for Christianity became very different. In the course of time the Western church ceased to orientate itself on the Roman emperor and empire, but because of the new conditions, with new powers, and for missionary motives, it turned westwards. The churches in East and West began their separate ways, on the one hand to the early Byzantine period and on the other to the early Middle Ages in the West. The Middle Ages in Europe were then shaped by a Christianity which had gained its contours as a church under the influences of Roman late antiquity and Hellenism.

For Further Reading

Peter Brown, *The World of Late Antiquity*, Harcourt, Brace Jovanovich and Thames and Hudson 1971

Hans Freiherr von Campenhausen, *Ecclesiastical Authority and Spiritual Power in the Church of the First Three Centuries*, Stanford University Press and A.& C. Black 1969

Henry Chadwick, *The Early Church*, Pelican History of the Church Vol.1, Penguin Books 1968

W. H. C. Frend, *The Early Church*, SCM Press ³1991

W. H. C. Frend, *The Rise of Christianity*, Fortress Press and Darton, Longman and Todd 1984

A. H. M. Jones, *The Later Roman Empire 284–602*, University of Oklahoma Press and Blackwell 1964

R. A. Markus, *Christianity in the Roman World*, Thames and Hudson 1974 and Scribners 1975

F. van Meer and C. Mohrmann, *Atlas of the Early Christian World*, Nelson 1958

J. Stevenson, *A New Eusebius*, SPCK ²1987 (revised by W. H. C. Frend)

J. Stevenson, *Creeds, Councils and Controversies*, SPCK ²1989 (revised by W. H. C. Frend)

Index of Names and Subjects